How To Use Generational Wisdom
to Grow Your Resilience

Built to
Thrive

MARY-JO BATHE

Published and printed by Ignite Publishing a division of Ignite YOU inc.
Canada, T4N1S1
Cover design by Brent Casteling
Book design by JB Owen and Kristine Magno
Edited by JB Owen, Mimi Safiyah, Lisa Mathew, and Carissa Simpson.
Designed in Canada, Printed in China
ISBN: 979-8-9910888-6-2
First edition:© November 2025

Ordering Information: Quantity sales. Special discounts are available on quantity purchases by corporations, associations, and others. For details, contact the publisher at the above address. Programs, products, or services provided by the author can be found by contacting them directly. Resources named in the book are found in the resources pages at the back of the book.

Author Information
Mary-Jo Bathe
Cobourg, ON
K9A 1P6
Canada
mjbathe107@gmail.com
maryjo@builttothrive.living

Instagram is a trademark of Meta Platforms, Inc.

Dedication

I dedicate this memoir to my father. You built more than houses, you helped me build the philosophy that guides my life.

I remember the soft rustle of your morning paper, the warmth of our breakfast shared in silence, and the effortless peace of two souls content to sit side by side. As a young girl, I became your trusty sidekick, makeshift secretary, and companion on the dusty roads between construction sites. I discovered how responsibility, humour, and heart could all fit in a single workday.

I can still feel the heat of the sauna and how your songs and stories rose with the steam. In the warm glow, you revealed how strength blooms in small gestures, how work increases with care, how generosity flows like water, and how happiness inspires open arms. You taught me how resilience grows in an unhurried moment when nurtured by a job well done and how kindness enhances joy when offered freely.

You lived by two simple truths: *Fear no man and nine out of ten things you worry about will never happen.* Your words guided me toward courage and away from doubt.

Today, when I dance, I feel your steady presence guiding my steps. When I am flustered, your strength allows me to soften, breathe, and remember what truly matters. The foundation you built still stands strong today, rooted in our family, in the hearts shaped by your tenderness, and in the lives forever touched by your love. Your tenacity, values, and unwavering optimism continue to carry us all forward.

Love You Dad,
Mary-Jo

Acknowledgements

Built to Thrive

*B*uilt *to Thrive* exists because of the love, wisdom, and unwavering support of the people who deepened my understanding of thriving and resilience as essential parts of a meaningful life.

To **Lady JB Owen,** thank you for being a living reminder that courage and kindness can change lives. Your unwavering strength in what's possible and your gift for helping me turn my personal resilience stories into collective resilience have helped me see that resilience is about igniting hope in others. Your assistance has empowered me to integrate my feminine energy and business savvy into my debut novel and has also helped me provide my memoir a generational story focus by creating structure and meaning around real-life events. JB places strong emphasis on community and legacy, which aligns perfectly with my desire to transmit generational wisdom. She is a tremendous mentor and friend.

I dedicate this book to my dad. A real man inspired the book. He was also a son, a grandson, a husband, a brother, an uncle, and a devoted dad. He was the kind of person who took responsibility, rarely voiced complaints, and simply completed tasks motivated by life's necessities. As his daughter, I am sharing the real-life moments I experienced through him. I believe that by sharing Dad's real-life periods of grit and lived experiences, there is something valuable for everyone to learn from his life. The moments of resilience he instilled in me continue to guide my daily life. Today, resilience holds as much importance as in the past, forming the foundation of strength that rises when most needed. Through his life experiences, Dad instilled in me inner strength, bravery, and drive that permeated his everyday routine. As his eldest daughter, I carry priceless moments of serenity. Perseverance, like a hidden strength, will support me when life challenges me. They become the silent axis and pivot points of my life's path.

To my **mom**, you are the foundation upon which this entire book stands. The wisdom and love you passed down, often expressed through quiet action, rather than words, revealed the essence of generational strength and wisdom. You taught about strength through flexibility, the power of hope in difficult seasons, and the importance of honouring earlier generations while creating something lasting for those who followed. Your resilience fills every page, and I remain endlessly grateful for the legacy you continue to build.

To my **husband, Michael**, you are both my anchor and my wings. Through long days, late nights of writing, moments of doubt, and sudden breakthroughs, your faith in my work never wavered. Your patience, encouragement, and quiet strength created the space for deep exploration and reflection within me. You show me every day how resilience and patience transform into love and action. Thank you for being with me every step of the way.

To my **brothers and sisters,** thank you for being my first teachers in connection, compassion, and the beautiful complexity of family. You've celebrated triumphs and offered support through challenges, and it reminded me that thriving is *never* solitary. As a writer and as a person, I have learned to use laughter, shared memories, and the hard-earned lessons of our struggles in my writing. I am who I am because of the bond we share.

To my **children and grandchildren**, you are my greatest joy and deepest purpose. Every word written is *yours*. May you come to know the stories of ancestors who came before, the strength flowing through your veins, and the wisdom carried across generations. You represent the living continuation of a legacy grounded in resilience and love. As you grow, dream, and create your own paths, my heart fills with hope for everything you will build and pass forward. You are built to thrive, not only to endure but also to flourish. You embody my legacy and are my most precious gift.

To my **friends**, thank you for surrounding me with laughter, truth, and love. Your support reminded me that thriving begins in the company of kind hearts.

To my **life coach and chiropractor,** your advice and guidance have helped me heal and grow in ways once unimaginable. You taught me to listen closely to my body, honour my journey, and understand that true resilience arises from harmony between mind, body, and spirit. Your insight helped me live the principles now shared within these pages.

To my **yoga teachers**, you revealed how strength and softness can coexist, how breath sustains us through uncertainty, and how simply showing up, day after day, becomes an act of thriving. Lessons learned on the mat now weave through my writing and daily life.

Finally, to **everyone** who shared a story, a struggle, or a triumph, your courage shines through every chapter. *Built to Thrive* stands as a testament to the power of shared wisdom and a celebration of resilience found in ordinary, yet extraordinary lives. Thank you for trusting me with your truth.

With deepest gratitude and love,
Mary-Jo

Built to *Thrive*

Preface

Why I Wrote This Book

What follows is a defining moment I have rarely spoken about. The surfacing of my wisdom, inner knowing, and resilience, fueled by my desire to thrive, not just survive, all rose to the surface. This powerful breakthrough ultimately inspired me to dig deep and fully embrace my full potential.

I still vividly remember the day I walked into my local women's shelter with just two suitcases full of my entire life's possessions, leaving twenty-six years of marriage and a house. I knew I had to go, not to escape abuse, but to break free from the life that had become a confining existence. I was uncertain and had more questions than answers.

Thankfully, I left with a quiet faith that I could get back on my feet. I had found a nearby women's shelter that would take me, as I had nowhere else to go. My new 'start' was a very small room with a bed, a desk, and a communal bathroom. The place offered not only a roof but also a lifeline that was entirely mine. From that small space, I began to piece together a new life, discovering strength I didn't know I had, and gathering the hope I knew I had lost. This small, tiny, basic room served as a lifeline and provided me with a place to start over.

On the first, second, and third nights, I softly sobbed. I was afraid someone would hear me, and I certainly didn't want anyone to realize how broken I was. However, amidst the tears and sorrow, I recalled my dad's words, *"The sun will rise, and the sun will set, and another day will come."* Just as Dad had said, *mornings came,* I woke up, and *life continued.*

At first, survival was the *only* goal. A great deal of effort went into eating, finding rest, and moving through the panic. However, one morning I woke up and noticed that I was no longer simply getting by. Brick by brick, day by ugly, glorious day, I had begun to rebuild. My transformation was unfolding, not as a dramatic discovery, but rather as a subtle awakening.

Early days at the women's shelter taught me that redefining one's life doesn't come easily. Strength is necessary, and resilience is mandatory. Every day had moments when life stripped away what once seemed essential, leaving me with only my deepest self. In those quiet moments of inner reflection, I began to hear the echoes and feel the threads of inherited strength woven from my dad's steady determination, my mother's quiet courage, and the unspoken wisdom of generations before me. I recalled stories my parents had shared that gave me renewed strength, and principles they instilled that inspired me to persevere. Each enduring hardship or unrelenting test I went through caused me to lean on their words, reminding me there's always a way through, even in the hardest chapters of one's life.

Quickly, I saw firsthand how the life I decided to rebuild could be richer, truer, and more my own. The wisdom within their many stories was the motivation that pushed me to carry on.

I'll admit that every step I took forward scraped something off me. Things I once valued, I knew I would never acquire back. I found out that sometimes life looks like *only two suitcases and a changed set of locks,* and that survival isn't always pretty or kind. Pain began to teach me things that comfort never would. I had no plan, no certainty, and a lot of sadness. However, amidst the overwhelming fear and grief, something began to unfold. A tiny, stubborn piece of me still believed in a different kind of life. The only certainty I had that more was possible was the solid foundation of truth and teachings provided by my parents.

I recall a frigid winter morning when the pipes in one of Dad's houses burst. He was already exhausted, up before dawn, hands raw from working in the cold, but Dad didn't hesitate. He grabbed his tools and fixed the frozen pipes. There were no complaints, no drama, just quiet determination.

When I was younger, I didn't understand the pressure he was under, but watching him that morning, trudging through the snow to repair what was broken, I recognized his endurance and refusal to give up, no matter how tired or tested he was. My parents showed me that purpose doesn't pause when life becomes challenging. Their exceptional support had imparted crucial life lessons I could depend on during the most challenging period of my life.

I'll admit, shaping a new beginning for myself happened gradually. I slowly rebelled through quiet acts of pushing back against the weight of the life I once knew. It seemed my parents' stories held me steady, and a small, stubborn spark ignited inside of me as I began to grow into my new life. My effort wasn't much at the start, but enough of me felt a flicker of hope to build a better future. I began to look for new tools and ideas. I found a book in the women's shelter library called *Ignite Forgiveness*. It was a collection of stories about people who chose to forgive themselves and others, and their lives changed as a result. The stories of everyday people overcoming their personal pain spoke directly to my heart and started to liberate me from my shadows. Before long, I found myself back in the library, immersed in *Ignite Wisdom*, another anthology brimming with personal tales of how wisdom and inner knowing transformed a person's life for the better.

Those two IGNITE™ books brought back memories of simpler times in my life, when my dad taught me commonplace skills and how to embody personal values. He had always encouraged me to dig deep and use the guiding lights of resilience, wisdom, and forgiveness to pick myself back up, reclaim my worth, and build a life where I could thrive. His constant teachings and helpful stories made me realize that the lessons we need to learn often come from within ourselves and from the wisdom passed down through the ages. He shared how *victories are born from adversity, turning points reshape lives, and wisdom is a profound reflection that reverberates throughout the generations.* He proved how stories stay with you, shape you, and remind you of your potential. He showed me how resilience helps you overcome life's difficulties so that you can succeed with a stronger, more stable foundation.

Those stories and the wisdom my father so graciously cultivated in me propelled my journey forward.

Rebuilding Myself

As I was reevaluating my life at the shelter, I discovered how pride can cloud perception and judgment, creating a fog that obscures clear thinking and genuine self-awareness. I was experiencing this firsthand. I was stressed, drained, and numb; I worried about everything. Still, I got up, if only to sit on the edge of the bed and catch my breath, tiny step by tiny step. Eventually, things began to get better, and I started to feel less alone and angry. I was also *more intuitive. More inclined. More connected to what I inherently possessed.* I remained hopeful and drew on my faith and conviction to keep going. I allowed myself to sit with discomfort, process the anger, cry when needed, and then celebrate the small victories I could achieve. Anger is often a secondary emotion hiding pain, fear, or a sense of injustice. At the same time, I allowed myself to embody my father's lessons and to trust the wisdom he had instilled, while nurturing the strength I was slowly reclaiming. And over time, a voice spoke up, telling me to *write a book.*

The truth is, I had been considering writing this book for a long time. Even before my new beginning, I loved witnessing powerful, inspiring, *everyday* instances of resilience, success, and perseverance in both business and life. The triumphs and epiphanies that emerged from significant life-changing moments captivated me. I knew that tenacity is a trait you can learn, grow, and sustain over time. I was sure that if you got up every day and were true to yourself, you'd rise.

All of that inspired me to create a book that serves as a *roadmap for rebuilding a better life*, rather than just a reflection on survival.

I want to reveal that life's most debilitating moments often contain significant, time-honoured knowledge. Deeply personal transformation becomes lived testimony, and the wisdom we desperately seek is *already within us.*

My goal in writing this book is to honour the resilience we all carry and showcase the legacy of the lessons handed down to me. In the current era, with the fading of generational wisdom today, I feel compelled to share my father's many lessons with you, allowing their inherent beauty to flourish. For those times when life is hard, when you feel alone, scared, or even uncertain, this book holds a truth you can count on, invest in, and use to bolster yourself back up through adversity.

Despite how difficult my shelter days were to discuss, I've found that my journey mirrors countless others. The line between our stories is veil-thin. We all face challenging times, difficult decisions, and painful events. Yet I have witnessed powerful moments of perseverance and dedication, where people have endured and overcome, only to emerge stronger. I have witnessed individuals thrive despite their circumstances. I have observed individuals conquer impossible odds because they reached deep within to pull something forth.

I wrote each chapter from a place of genuine strength, *even though life still hurts from time to time.* The shelter wasn't a failure; it was proof of the fight *still alive within me.* The life unfolding wasn't what I had envisioned, yet it felt real, *truly mine,* and for the first time, *enough.*

What I know is that if we access what's within us, we *will* find the answers we seek.

After everything, *I am still here,* standing strong, thanks to the generational wisdom and love of my parents, in particular my father, who supported me and taught me so much.

I share this to light the way and help others wanting to find their footing.

You have this strength *within* you, ready to be discovered. You *can* achieve everything you desire and so much more when you realize you were *Built to Thrive.*

Peace and joy. Be well,
Mary-Jo

Contents

Dedication iii

Acknowledgements v

Built to Thrive v

Preface xi

Why I Wrote This Book xi

Introduction xxi

Thriving In Life . . . . **xxi**

PART 1: BUILDING YOUR LIFE 1

Chapter One: How This Book Will Support You 3

Chapter Two: Why Read On 11

Chapter Three: Built By Example 19

Chapter Four: The House We Built 25

Chapter Five: Breaking Ground 35

Chapter Six: Foundation of Strength 47

Chapter Seven: Framing the Structure 59

Chapter Eight: Opening Windows and Doors 71

Chapter Nine: Reframing & Renewal 81

Chapter Ten: Rest & Repair 93

PART 2: THRIVING IN LIFE **109**

Chapter Eleven: Beyond Survival 111

Chapter Twelve: The Art of Contentment 125

Chapter Thirteen: Thriving Through Connection 137

Chapter Fourteen: Generational Thriving 151

Chapter Fifteen: Living with Purpose & Meaning 163

Chapter Sixteen: The Daily Practice of Thriving 179

PART 3: REFLECTION & APPLICATION **195**

Chapter Seventeen: Your Resilience Reflections 197

Chapter Eighteen: Knowing Your Resilience Strengths . . . 217

Chapter Nineteen: Building Your Personal Blueprint 231

Chapter Twenty: The Legacy of Thriving 255

Final Reflection: A Final Word 263

Epilogue: Coming Home 265

About the Author 267

Book Resource List 269

Introduction

Thriving In Life

There's a wonderful reason you're holding this book in your hands. I believe it's because you might crave something engaging, captivating, relevant, compelling, and full of poignant life lessons. *You are not alone.*

Let's be honest: today, most information feels disposable rather *than* relatable. We scroll endlessly, click constantly, and chase updates that vanish as quickly as they appear, leaving us feeling misinformed and disconnected. But when I recall the wisdom my father shared with me, what my elders taught me, and the resilience instilled in me through real-life stories, it feels different. *That stays.* Resilience and generational wisdom intertwine to demonstrate the transmission of knowledge, strength, and coping skills over time. People have lived, tested, and carried this wisdom from one generation to the next, even in the face of modern technology. That's why preserving these stories matters deeply. Words and memories become blueprints of resilience, quiet lessons of survival, and timeless reminders of what *it truly means to live with purpose.*

Every one of us can build a resilient life. The best place to start is with the wisdom you have, and allow the beauty behind it to flourish. For those times when life is hard, when you feel alone, scared, or even uncertain, this book holds a truth you can count on, invest in, and use to bolster yourself back up through adversity.

Drawing on my father's journey and the hard-won knowledge he relied on to keep himself and our family going, I wrote this book to share wisdom and resilience you can draw upon when you need them most because...

Wisdom is earned and learned through tears and triumph.

Thriving Joyously

We all face challenging times, difficult decisions, and painful events. Yet I have witnessed powerful moments of perseverance and dedication that people have endured and overcome, only to emerge stronger. I have watched individuals thrive despite their circumstances. I have observed others conquer impossible odds because inner strength has always been there, growing inside us through every hardship. Each morning we rise, and each time we choose hope over despair, we build something within us. Resilience and small victories already exist, even if our awareness has not yet experienced them.

The truth is, we all face moments when life demands more from us than we think we have to give. *You may have suffered a setback in your career. A relationship may have ended. A loss may have occurred, changing everything.* These are the moments that test us, that strip away everything we thought was essential and leave us wondering if we have what it takes. This book exists to overcome exactly those moments and to help you enjoy the life you're ready to enjoy on the other side of them.

Having lived for over six decades on this earth, I've learned that safeguarding generational wisdom ensures that enduring truth continues to shape lives across time. Your life is 'Built to Thrive' because of the tenacity of your generational heritage. You now get to carry that on.

In writing this book, I poured my heart and soul into something I believe will resonate with you. My stories of tenacity and silent resistance contain wisdom and reflect perspectives gained from lived experiences, developed over many generations. These reflections on the past will take you on a journey rich with moments both entertaining and deeply meaningful. This kind of wisdom can change your life and give you the confidence you need to move forward.

I am delighted to say that 'Built to Thrive' is part memoir, part practical guide, and part love letter to the resilience and quiet victories within all of us. It is a tribute to a generation that knew true hardship and a guide for those of today who desire more than comfort and convenience. This book is for anyone who values nostalgia, welcomes commitment, appreciates sharing, support, and personal growth.

This book is a tale of triumph, breakthroughs, tenacity, and even 'stubborn' resilience, intended for anyone who wants to learn how to solve the issues in their life today with grace and endurance. We are all at different places in our journey, but this is for anyone seeking transformative answers at any stage.

I believe wisdom is universal, available, and just waiting to be used, and that thriving is more than just getting by or surviving. Living life to the fullest means growing, developing, and succeeding, often despite life's obstacles and barriers. Drawing on your personal strengths is the key to transitioning from survival mode to *genuine happiness*.

There is a wonderful reason you are holding this book in your hands: it will help you honour your well-being, reach your full potential, and experience genuine happiness, success, and contentment as you prosper and flourish. You are likely ready to access your wisdom, learn new things, and discover the gifts inside of you that have been passed down by your family, your ancestors, and humanity.

Savour this moment.

Enjoy the experience.

You were, without a doubt, *Built to Thrive*.

Let's begin.

PART 1:

BUILDING YOUR LIFE

Every lasting structure begins the same way: with intention, planning, and the courage to break ground. Before walls rise, before windows open, before life fills the rooms, there must be a foundation strong enough to hold what comes next.

The same is true for your life. The values you root yourself in. The boundaries you establish. The habits you practice when no one's watching. The relationships you tend. The way you process difficulty. These become the unseen architecture of resilience.

Part One is about laying that groundwork. You'll learn to break ground on new beginnings, pour foundations strong enough to hold your dreams, frame your life with intention, and create the structural integrity that lets you weather any storm. This work isn't glamorous. It often happens in quiet moments, small decisions, and unglamorous effort that no one sees.

The work begins here. With breaking ground, trusting the process, and believing that what you build, layer by careful layer, will be strong enough to hold not just survival, but the full, thriving life you're meant to live.

Let's build.

How This Book Will Support You

Stories Are Golden

Like many of us, you might be at a place in your life where you are seeking a guide or lifeline to help you find more excitement, comfort, support, solace, and peace within your heart. Perhaps life has delivered you challenges or struggles, and you need inspiration and insights to awaken a greater understanding.

The perspectives presented in this book include not only my own but also those of my father, his father, my mother, and her mother. Many have come from my grandparents. The generational wisdom they represent has helped me throughout my life, and now it may help you view your own family's wisdom in a new light. My hope is you will find the answers to the questions you've carried for years. You'll uncover deeper enlightenment, richer healing, and spark inspiration, determination, or insight to help you realize that *you already have what you need inside of you to live a successful, dynamic, and vibrant life.*

Many people find themselves seeking purpose, community, sound judgment, blessings, and success after experiencing setbacks or roadblocks imposed by external forces. Others find solace in activities such as meditation, art, spending time in nature, or revisiting significant memories. I enjoy all of these, but find that *stories of profound transformation* help us better navigate our lives by revealing the inner strength, courage, and power that are inherently instilled within.

Most stories emphasize values like accountability, perseverance, and dedication, while showing intrinsic qualities that help enhance our lives. Reading these stories gives us comfort in knowing that we're not alone in our struggles. They often offer practical guidance for negotiating both calm and turbulent waters when life can feel overwhelming.

In my own moments of struggle, returning to simpler times when things were less difficult and distressing provided comfort in my life. Growing up in the 1960s and 1970s, life was changing quickly, especially during the Women's Liberation Movement, when women were achieving gender equality in the social, political, and economic spheres. Women, no longer limited to childcare and housework, were advocating for shared domestic responsibilities and personal autonomy. The approach was a departure from gender norms. The principles my parents shared and my adaptations of them sparked something deep inside of me, shifting my definition of success and fulfilment and keeping me grounded in what truly matters.

My upbringing placed great focus on the value of family, common sense, and modest living. As a child, my father taught me the values of discipline, hustle, hard work, self-control, perseverance, tenacity, and elbow grease. My strength has grown from those early lessons and stories, which offered a sense of support I can always lean on in difficult times.

Long after growing up, I still carry Dad's voice, teachings, and sense of security within me, drawing on his guidance when needed most. I felt extremely vulnerable and alone when I lived in the shelter, but something held despite the emptiness. Eventually, I was able to rediscover how to live and love again after giving up everything I owned to survive.

My dad's traditional steadfastness served as a roadmap for navigating the commotion of life. I soon realized that not just me, but *everyone* could learn from his calm determination, silent strength, and positive attitude that reflected his inner resilience. The resilience of Dad's 'Silent Generation' demonstrates how to navigate the challenges of the contemporary world and how inherited knowledge can support each of us during our own trying times.

Resilience Is Key

This book will help you learn what my dad taught me. Your greatest strength lives within you. You'll discover how to realize your potential, believe in your ability, and face life's obstacles with alertness and purpose by hearing about my personal odyssey and the values that changed my life. These pages will empower you to use your inner strength and optimistic outlook to navigate life with inner calm and purpose. We all need to cultivate the capacity for resilience within ourselves.

My goal is that the stories and wisdom in these pages will transform how you see yourself and relate to others. Through each example, you'll recognize your own capacity for self-assurance, potential, and willpower. These 'soul print' stories of effort and triumph invite you to reimagine what your successes and setbacks really mean.

Before long, you'll begin to notice your own moments of resilience. You'll catch a glimpse of your own highs and lows and see how life's chaotic and jumbled obstacles, failures, and aspirational objectives reflect the resilience you already possess. Hearing the stories and wisdom that connect the past, present, and future provides us with a feeling of continuity and direction.

A stronger, wiser, and more genuine version of yourself is waiting to shine on the other side of life's chaos. Whether you laugh, cry, or simply sigh deeply, I hope what you read here gives you the courage and self-compassion to face your fears. The true victory for you will be if these pages spark a glimmer of joy, sharpness, or "*Hey, maybe I can as well.*" I want these candid, hopeful moments to serve as a reminder that strength doesn't always mean winning. Sometimes we endure, sometimes we adapt, and sometimes we just survive, and that's enough. Life's wisdom isn't about becoming invincible but rather about showing up regardless of the outcome.

CHAPTER ONE: HOW THIS BOOK WILL SUPPORT YOU

Life is filled with joy, pleasure, and challenges. Our beliefs about our jobs, relationships, finances, health, families, and self-worth fit into our life story, and the knowledge we gain from family memories empowers us. Reading about hardship, heartbreak, history, and hope makes us feel a certain way and reminds us that no matter how far you fall, there is always a way back up. Despite life's challenges, you can overcome them and succeed in both your business and your personal life. All we need is a little courage, a lot of determination, and some life lessons from those who have already experienced the challenging path.

Thriving Within You

Everything I have written here is intended to open your eyes (and your heart) to the true beauty and strength of human resilience. After reading, I hope you feel empowered, inspired, and valued. The stories on these pages are based on the actual experiences of regular people travelling on real journeys. Each chapter provides a window into the past, where frank communication and blunt honesty blended with unwavering fortitude prevailed. The aim is to comprehend current and generational struggles and transform them into personal victories. Here, sincere dialogue and unwavering tenacity mix to make sense of both historical hardships and contemporary chaos, and transform them into individual victories.

While I encourage you to find your own inner resilience, stillness, and tranquillity, I also wish you to see the blessings in your story.

Take stock, find peace, and enjoy comfort in the wisdom your life has created. Perhaps your story and learning will help someone you know experience more in their life journey. Your words will open their hearts and eyes to the amazing resilience of the human spirit and remind them that success and perseverance are both possible.

We can all learn valuable life lessons by reflecting on the past and applying the transformative power of tenacity to our everyday lives. The world is in desperate need of stories of intergenerational hope and lessons from our ancestors during difficult times. I want to reach people looking for a strong, inspirational book or those seeking an intimate, truthful, and inspiring journey. Stepping forward with a relentless tenacity in their brightest and darkest moments, drawn from testimonies of courage, ingenuity, flexibility, awakening, and transformation. These are not solely my own personal experiences. These memories reveal the possibilities that come when we don't let our darkest moments define who we are.

Learning about individuals who have overcome adversity demonstrates the true strength and resilience of the human spirit. Life will knock you down, but *you can get back up and win.*

You will become stronger by drawing on your inner strength.

This material will make you laugh, maybe shed a tear or two, and give you the extra courage and strength to face your fears head-on. May you find peace in your own life, as my dad did, by remembering your inner willpower. As you discover hidden qualities such as strength and resilience, *you're ensuring you're on the right path.*

I hope that as you read, you'll feel a connection within yourself and with the generations whose voices echo through these words. You might want to share them with those you care about, like I did, so these stories continue to live on in other people's hearts.

CHAPTER TWO

Why Read On

Unlock the Timeless Wisdom of Resilience

Now that you understand how this book will support you, you might be wondering *why* I have chosen resilience as the key characteristic in thriving throughout your life.

I believe that resilience represents the human capacity to navigate life's highs and lows, endure storms, and emerge stronger on the other side. The path is rarely easy, yet having resilience shapes our identity and fuels our *recovery*. Resilience necessitates our dedication and perseverance, even in the face of life's most severe challenges. The most devoted soul repeatedly strengthens their resilience to rise after a setback, learn from mistakes, and find the strength to ask for help from others.

Most of us can agree that resilience never calls for the denial of pain or the pretence of perfection. Instead, resilience equips us with the tools we need to heal and regain our footing after life's disappointments. It enables us to persevere through difficulties and rise again after disaster or loss. The resilient journey involves feeling the hurt and *choosing* to continue anyway. Each step requires us to draw on our inner resources, such as humour, adaptability, confidence, and a desire to rebuild from within.

When tough or unwanted emotions arise, resilience enhances our ability to process them, intensifying the experience, gaining new insights, and raising our awareness of what more we can accomplish.

Many of us fail to see our unwavering resilience and perseverance as our most powerful weapon against adversity. We do not consider ourselves resilient, and thus, we struggle to meet the demands of life.

However, by learning how to activate resilience, we teach ourselves how to overcome challenges and thrive in the face of adversity. We strengthen and improve our mental fortitude, inner conviction, and adaptability to stand firm and maintain our footing in the midst of calamity or hardship.

I made resilience the focus and emphasis of this book because of the value it brings and because each of us *already* possesses the resilience we require to live our best and greatest lives.

Building Resilience Markers

Building one's resilience is the process of gaining the ability to adapt, recover, and grow stronger in the face of test of strength, stress, and trauma.

I've realized that awareness reveals options and empowers choices, which serve as the foundation of resilience. It also has enormous power by opening up possibilities, reducing self-judgment, and activating our problem-solving intellect. Asking the appropriate questions in challenging situations reveals hidden jewels and creates what I call positive *strength patterns*.

Consider *strength patterns* your personal building procedures, the strategies you've learned for developing a strong foundation, reinforcing weak points, and creating a life *built to last*. When faced with a challenge, you return to these approaches. Similar to muscle memory, these patterns automatically activate when challenges arise, enabling you to navigate with a familiar ease. As you create these new *strength patterns*, you *increase* your resilience. When someone around you lost control, *did you stay calm, think creatively, adjust to the situation,* or *simply listen well?* Such responses create a feedback cycle, revealing your *strength patterns* and increasing resilience both *inside* yourself and in the *work* around you.

Unfortunately, when you're in crisis or caught in a habit, old coping mechanisms tend to kick in. Frequently, our *strength patterns* deteriorate, and we lose our ability to progress. That moment is a cue to *pause, ponder,* and *reconnect* with our inner resilience. The first step is always to become aware of oneself and reflect. Then, by acknowledging the situation, you can actively slow down or simply admit that being stuck is transient and temporary, *even if* your feelings indicate otherwise.

My own life's difficulties forced me to establish numerous helpful *strength patterns*, which resulted in something fantastic. They activated powerful new *resilience markers* that facilitated positive changes in complex areas of my life: family dramas, difficult life lessons, and personal disappointments. Those new *resilience markers* served as the foundation for more cohesive decisions and empowered me to overcome external obstacles by tapping into what I *already* had on the inside. When I regained strength, *resilience markers* became my 'collective intelligence,' which enhanced and cultivated my inner resilience.

When it comes to the foundation of life, consider *resilience markers* as indicators of structural integrity. They demonstrate proof that what you've built *can* withstand and endure pressure, the same as walls that hold strong, roofs that don't leak during storms, and foundations that *don't* crack when stressed.

Resilience markers can also aid us in discovering our true selves. These markers appear when we conquer obstacles and work our way through them. Each *resilience marker* we develop increases our self-assurance and motivation to thrive and accomplish again and again.

Resilience markers can frequently divert our journey and teach us valuable lessons that alter the course of our lives. Most *resilience markers* provide feedback by retaining our sense of clarity under pressure, measuring reasonability during stressful times, or even finding moments of delight when faced with excessive stress. They're the signs that tell you your coping systems are functioning and you are not simply surviving.

Your *resilience markers* are life's subtle signs that you're managing stress well. Consider the personal traits, rituals, and inner qualities that have helped you overcome adversity in the past. These same qualities and inclinations are present now, assisting you to persevere, endure, and *never* give up. These abilities are precisely what will assist you in discovering the *resilience markers* that exist within you.

What I want you to realize is that building and developing resilience does not imply becoming someone new. It's about understanding your inner strengths and learning how to use them more consciously and intentionally.

As you read the stories in this book, you will become more aware of your own patterns and markers. You'll understand and realize why certain problems seem easier to navigate than others. You'll learn to trust yourself more deeply. You will realize how your 'strength patterns' are the strategies that have previously helped you get through difficult circumstances and challenging times. Your *resilience markers* demonstrate that those strategies *work*. Together, these elements create your personal toolkit not only for survival but also for thriving.

Learning Resilience From My Father

In my life, my father's inner focus and continued resilience taught me *appreciation* and *curiosity* for my *strength patterns* and *resilience markers*. He made it clear to me that employing both was a survival strategy as well as a form of self-awareness. He taught me to be receptive to what they had to teach me and to always ask myself continuous questions to further develop both of them. "Curiosity is a critical survival tool," he'd say, guiding me away from fear and toward possibilities during difficult times. "Appreciation is understanding everything is a gift," he'd say, encouraging me to live in appreciation and gratitude. By carefully evaluating my *strength patterns* and *resilience markers*, as Dad did, I discovered strategies to overcome the specific challenges life demanded of me.

Placing Dad at the core of my source of wisdom opened a doorway, providing access to his generational knowledge while also grounding my future in courage and relatability. Dad's capacity to apologize, forgive, and move on taught me that relationships can survive a rupture or breakdown. Dad expanded my capacity to see problems from different perspectives and adjust my thoughts as my circumstances changed. He freely admitted mistakes, modified his approach, and taught me mental agility. Dad balanced his life by building his independence, which strengthened and boosted his *resilience markers* and inspired me.

Today, focusing on both my *strength patterns* and *resilience markers* is a consistent, everyday practice that has strengthened my resolve, sharpened my intellect, and helped me reflect. It has enabled my life to *bloom*. Thriving has evolved beyond mere survival and become more than just getting by. Living life to the fullest means I am *growing, developing,* and *succeeding,* frequently in the face of snags and barriers. Using these two strategies has resulted in a magnificent turnaround and beautiful transformation in my life, shifting from 'getting by' to true success and well-being. Both have enabled me to attain my full potential and feel intellectually, emotionally, and physically fulfilled, successful, and pleased.

This book aims to teach you how to create your own *strength patterns* and *resilience markers*, helping you tap into your inner resilience to confront challenges head-on. The regular practices you learn here will help you build and develop resilience over time, eventually evolving into a new *superpower*.

Just like me, witnessing my dad's unrelenting resilience and unwavering persistence helped me to obtain insights into my inner strength and desired future; the upcoming chapters will help you obtain insights into your own growth and possibilities. These pages feature experiences and moments that evoke the resilience you need to attract *love*, build *empathy*, sense *exhilaration*, and *conquer* setbacks.

Resilience underpins the common sense lessons I teach, which improve your viewpoint and reinforce your values. Unlocking the timeless wisdom of resilience is a journey I take you on through previous generations, building on foundations laid long before our time. Understanding the past resilience and fortitude of individuals who have faced storms before us enables us to build on that strength and forge ahead. The resilience we learn, acquire, and receive from our ancestors serves as the foundation for all efforts throughout every stage of our lives.

Reading my stories and the ones I've witnessed will, in turn, bring you enormous victories and some truly lovely moments that are filled with humour and motivation to inspire you. You will most likely recognize aspects of yourself, find areas where you can thrive and flourish, and notice where you are *already* winning and succeeding in your life. Every emotion you feel in the chapters to come is a part of the experience, because authentic, unadorned memories of struggle and triumph help us discover and realize our own potential. This inner wealth and riches allow us to thrive in new and future activities.

Being open to discovery and exploration allows you to notice your own *resilience markers* and embrace and accept your *helpful and beneficial strength patterns*. Many people are unaware that they're already using these tools more effectively than they think. By actively pursuing processes and aligning with the pull of your own potential, you begin to find and activate your *strength patterns*, using them to *improve* and *enhance* your current situations.

Trust that the journey ahead will help you learn how tenacity, resilience, a bit of determination, and a whole lot of inner strength are your secret weapons when life throws you an unexpected twist. I hope this book and my father's lessons show you that you can succeed as you are. You only need to acknowledge what you already have inside you.

Your resilience has been building all along. Now it's time to use it intentionally.

CHAPTER THREE

Built By Example

A Father's Foundation

Before discussing the many examples, references, and ideology surrounding the *Built to Thrive* ideals, I want to highlight the person who exemplified them the most, my dad. This book wouldn't be what it is without the wisdom and wonder my father passed on to me. The relationship between the two of us has greatly influenced who I am and how I view the world. It has also taught me how to relate to my family, community, career, and personal development.

This book honours the generational resilience and ability to thrive through trying to diversify that he taught me until the day he passed away. He was like a bridge, spanning multiple generations, and serving as a mirror for me to view life from a more empowering perspective.

I hold deep respect for the kind of resilience forged by necessity, rather than by choice, in my father's generation. Necessity became my father's teacher, while circumstances served as his greatest opponent *and* guide. Dad's generation learned resilience through survival and created an unshakeable foundation of practical wisdom. He exemplified how creativity is born from limitation, and the ability to see potential where others see impossibility is a skill we can all learn and personify.

I now want to pass those valuable qualities on to you.

As a young child, I recall observing my dad's composed manner during many struggles. As his plumber's helper and mini-apprentice, I helped Dad by bringing him his tools while I watched him work. I would occasionally tighten a bolt while Dad's seasoned and worn hands skillfully fixed any broken items. Whether repairing a leaky roof during a storm, unclogging a toilet, or extending the life of his vintage company trucks, Dad exuded a confidence I admired but didn't fully understand at such a tender age.

Dad taught me that real strength isn't dramatic. Instead, it's the quiet determination to get up every day, keep going, finish the work at hand, and, despite the difficulties, build something important *one brick at a time*. Regardless of the circumstances, he'd look at our mess and say, *"Problems are just puzzles. You just need the right tools."* Decades passed before I realized Dad wasn't just talking about plungers, wrenches, and screwdrivers.

When resources were limited and the future was uncertain, Dad's common sense approach embodied the resilience and hard-earned generational wisdom of someone who had learned to discern between imagined and real problems. I quickly learned that he was the kind of person who was *Built to Thrive*, and any actions he took were meant to last. Dad always conserved his energy so he could direct it toward solving real issues rather than fighting shadows or facing the unseen.

Wisdom From the Past

My Dad, who was born during the Great Depression, carried himself with a quiet strength that came from having experienced real trials and tribulations since he was a young child. Imagine a boy who grew up during Canada's hardest economic years and emerged with an unfailing blueprint for turning resilience into a meaningful, prosperous family and business life. The roots of strength held Dad steady as he ascended through life's struggles. He was always able to pick up the pieces, piece by piece, dust himself off, and begin each day anew with the support of his own awareness of perseverance and resolve.

Growing up during the Great Depression, Dad was not given the option of giving up when things got tough. He learned how to take advantage of opportunities when they seemed unattainable, transform *nothing into something,* and work tirelessly to build a better future. His resilience was modest and understated. It came with steady daily action, not bold moves. Dad would often say to me and my friends, *"Nine out of ten things you worry about never happen,"* while grinning knowingly. His go-to phrase became more than a catchy saying; it became a staple in my consciousness. Over the years, I've shared that expression with my family and friends, transforming those words into a cornerstone of my mindset. I consider that strength his greatest inheritance, which he then passed on to me.

Dad's legacy of sharing memories and fostering resilience instilled the conviction that we have survived before and will survive again. Dad had faith in the slow, gradual bloom. He trusted the slow, unhurried process of development and change. Such trust requires self-compassion and a belief that something wonderful is occurring.

As I've grown older, I've come to understand the profound value of simple wisdom, particularly from a man who built everything from nothing. Dad's quiet teachings became the foundation I stand on today, and they're woven into every story you'll read in the pages ahead. What Dad built wasn't just a business or a life; it was a testament to what's possible when resilience meets determination. That's the foundation I want to pass on to you.

Learning Forward

Our culture is obsessed with finding quick fixes rather than accepting that slow growth is still real growth. In fact, the most profound changes often occur quietly, leaving us barely aware of them until we reflect on our own development. Healing, personal development, and growth can occur naturally over time, so significant changes don't have to be drastic or immediate.

I discovered such a deep resonance between my life experiences and Dad's practical wisdom that I found it impossible to ignore. His anecdotes about life became internal resources during my darkest moments, offering me a perspective I might not have had access to on my own. Dad encouraged independence and, combined with his balanced protection, allowed me to try new things and helped me develop self-efficacy, which grew into the belief that I *could* handle all that comes my way.

Dad taught me actual skills that made me more resilient and independent, from changing a tire to negotiating a salary. Dad shared intergenerational stories about his family history with me. His stories about overcoming tremendous obstacles still help me understand they're all part of a larger narrative of strength. My father was a master builder of a storm-resistant life, not just of walls and roofs. Dad profoundly shaped my ethical principles and my understanding of how to treat others and anticipate reciprocity. His stories about overcoming tremendous obstacles help me understand *we're all part of a larger narrative and that my foundation grows stronger by drawing from the collective.*

Looking back now, I can see that Dad was planting seeds that bloomed along the way, but I didn't recognize them until I had the life experience to understand their true meaning. Older generations share their tools and the approaches they used to overcome their challenges. Children learn how their elders survived and thrived. Lived examples teach resilience more powerfully than words alone.

I believe we all have people in our lives who share wisdom, ideals, and anecdotes, yet we don't always recognize their worth. That is why this book and the wisdom it shares mirror the fundamental messages about life, success, and happiness in ways that resonate deeply with everyone.

These lived examples teach resilience more powerfully than words alone. Often, seeds of wisdom are planted early in life and bloom all along, but we don't recognize their true meaning until we gain the *life experience* to fully understand them.

The stories and lessons throughout this book reflect the wisdom Dad instilled in me, and they're meant to help you recognize the wisdom *already* instilled in you. Your life is *Built to Thrive* because of the tenacity of your generational heritage, just as mine has been. You carry within you the strength, resilience, *and* practical wisdom of everyone who came before you.

The chapters ahead will help you see it, claim it, and use it intentionally.

You were *Built to Thrive.* Let me show you how.

CHAPTER FOUR

The House We Built

Why Building Became My Metaphor for Resilience in Life

As I started writing *Built to Thrive*, visions of a house under construction filled my mind. This was not just any house, but one where each beam, wall, and window fulfilled its purpose beautifully. Each aspect of the house was assembled with care, making a structure unlike any other: solid, reliable, long-lasting, and cherished.

As I thought about building a house, I saw how it resembled life. Life is something we create and shape over time, *planned but not perfect*, sometimes messy but always worthwhile.

Building a house requires time, effort, and patience. A home, like a person's life, evolves as goals shift, seasons change, and unforeseen challenges occur. The work forever continues, even as plans change.

For me, getting up every day and adding another brick, board, or creative touch to the 'home' that lives within me is mandatory. Each day brings new ideas and thoughts that grow in my heart and become aspects of the *sanctuary* I am creating.

I chose building as the central theme because the way we grow as individuals mirrors how structures grow. Every project begins with an idea, a dream, or a sketch that will eventually face the elements, time constraints, and pressures of the outside world. We can overcome outside forces as long as we are prepared and willing to rebuild, strengthen, mend, and restart. The way we tend to our home mimics the way we tend to our life: cherished or neglected, valued or abandoned.

Why I Chose Building as My Metaphor

My father's attitude toward the homes he worked in and the houses he helped construct inspired me to implement this element in this book. Every home he built and serviced reflected his perseverance and pride. He lived his life by building relationships and refusing to give up. He taught me that to build means to believe, to see potential where others do not, to measure twice and cut once, and to stick to the blueprint even when you think it might falter.

Building is about putting things in their proper place and giving them a reason to exist. It's creating order from chaos and *meaning* from materials. People have always aspired to improve what they have and leave something lasting for future generations. We build not just for ourselves but for *those who will walk through our doors long after we're gone.* Every structure we create, whether physical or emotional, becomes part of the landscape we pass forward. From ancient monuments to modern homes, from family traditions to business empires, we are driven to construct things that outlast us, that speak to who we are and what we value.

Dad built with the future in mind, knowing his children and grandchildren might one day walk across the floors he laid or open the doors he hung. That's the builder's gift: *creating today what will matter tomorrow.* When my Dad built houses, he never expected them to be perfect from the start. He anticipated improvement and growth. Dad understood that creating things well required time, care, and the ability to adapt. Weather could delay the foundation pour, or a wall might need squaring, but none of these eventualities would deter him because they were simply part of the building process.

The House as a Picture of Self

Throughout this book, I use 'building' as a metaphor for life. Every home has more than just walls and a roof. It embodies structure, order, warmth, and community. Every nail driven, each window set, and coat of paint represents a choice, a wish, and a deliberate plan for the life ahead.

Similarly, we build an 'inner' home, a life structure comprising of habits, values, relationships, and preferences. We don't build once and abandon it. As seasons change, we live in, maintain, and renovate it. We add wings of knowledge and porches where we can rest; we refurbish, renovate, tear down, and build back up again. Life's storms might rip off a few tiles or shake the structure, yet all the while, it is simply revealing what is stable and strong deep within.

A house can be beautiful without being immaculate, and a life doesn't have to be perfect to be meaningful and valuable. We also build internal belief systems, routines, and values, and whether we realize it or not, we live inside what we've built. Some parts *serve us well*. Others wear out. Over time, we're forced to look at what's holding us together and what needs reinforcing.

Just like a real house, the structure of a life can weaken, shift, or even collapse. But that doesn't mean it's beyond repair. It means it's time to rebuild even stronger, smarter, and more aligned with who we've become.

Every sturdy house needs these core elements. The same is true for us.

The Foundation:
- is our character, which serves as the moral ground on which we stand, providing us support.

The Frame:
- represents our boundaries, choices, and responsibilities, showing our limits and duties.

The Walls:
- offer protection and definition, regulating what we let in and what we keep out.

The Windows:
- provide perspective by allowing light in and altering our view of the world.

The Roof:
- keeps us safe during storms, our strength layered like shingles to protect us when life becomes tough.

The Doors:
- show when to open, when to close, and when to rebuild, representing transformation, change, risk, and connection.

The building metaphor reminds us that creating something meaningful and living it fully takes time and devotion.

Building as a Problem-Solving Strategy

You can see how each part of the structure plays a role in our lives, both internally and externally. The work never starts with finished rooms or smooth walls. It begins in the dirt. The first dig is rarely exciting. Dust rises, the ground pushes back, and there is little to show for it. But even in that mess, something important is taking shape. The foundation is forming where no one can see it yet. This inner work is essential, as it shapes character, commitment, and clarity through the process of building.

Too often, we see life's challenges as problems requiring solutions. But a builder has a different perspective. A builder views a crack in the wall as an opportunity to reinforce it. A delay is a chance to create better arrangements. A storm serves as a reminder to fix the drains next time.

To build something meaningful, you must solve difficulties by giving them purpose. It requires the capacity to transform challenges into opportunities for growth.

Repair as Renewal

In building and construction, repair does not mean failure. Repair shows you have lived well, as your home has served, protected, and supported you.

Homes show distress because people live in them. Materials shift, settle, and breathe. *Life is the same.* Distress in our hearts builds over time from loss, pain, or disappointment. However, these cracks teach us to strengthen our structure by incorporating the core components we need.

My father used to say, "*A good builder doesn't curse a leak; he repairs it.*" That simple truth shapes how I approach my life. Every repair we complete improves our preparedness for future storms.

Building Together

Nobody builds alone. Architects, carpenters, electricians, and plumbers all collaborate to build a house, each bringing distinct talents. Life is the same way. Our families, friends, teachers, and communities help *shape who we are.*

Thriving in life is a group effort. Sharing the load makes us all stronger. My Dad used to say that every generation adds a new room to the home of stories and legacy. Our parents constructed the house, we built the walls, and our children open new doors and create new opportunities. See your challenges as opportunities to repair or renovate. Pick up your tools; you're about to learn, and remember that your efforts strengthen the house we call life.

Resilience as the Roof

If life is like a house, resilience acts as the roof, keeping us safe and dry during storms. Rain doesn't stop falling, but a good roof teaches us how to stay dry while it does. The roof may not be the most visually appealing aspect of the house, but it plays a crucial role during adverse weather.

Resilience develops over time, much like shingles are layered one by one. Daily actions, like showing up, seeking support, and engaging in hopeful behaviours, all help build that quality. These layers protect you over time. A resilient life requires ongoing care and maintenance. It's a life that endures because we continuously repair and improve it.

The Living Blueprint

If we are living, we are *always* building. Our 'life blueprints' adapt, evolve, and change as we do. The foundation we poured years ago may require reinforcement. We may need to repurpose old rooms for something new. When we embrace change, we fortify our exterior, acknowledging that, akin to construction, we are perpetually unfinished.

When I think of my father, I remember someone who understood the need for self-improvement. He never rushed his work, kept his hands steady, and maintained firm faith while learning more about himself and life. Yes, he built houses, but more importantly, he built hope.

The Pulse of Building

Breaking ground, laying foundations, framing walls, opening windows, and *installing doors* are all stages of the *Built to Thrive* ideology. These elements embody how building one's life and fully thriving naturally transition from action to rest and from construction to completion.

Fully thriving is about aligning our lives with a harmonious rhythm so we can live long and well. We live best when we balance life's tempos, alternating between work, rest, and rejuvenation. We appreciate it more when we take action and then find time to enjoy ourselves. Both doing and pausing are needed to fully succeed.

At the end of each chapter, to ensure you are experiencing both the *push* and the *pull* life offers, you will find a place to pause, reflect, and assess your progress. Each chapter concludes with a *Thrive Principle*, *a brief reflection to help you move from outward creation to inward confirmation.*

Each principle is like a structural check for your life's *improvement.* They help you ask questions like, *"Is your foundation still strong?* *"Do you have solid support? Are you able to see outward clearly? Do you feel the right amount of light?"*

These sections realign your awareness to what matters most. We do not construct a life in a single step. We build in phases, through experience, reflection, and choices. We learn what holds and what falls apart, enough to reconstruct what matters, but it can take months or years to come up with ideas, consider what's possible, and muster the courage to start.

As you move forward, I encourage you to see what you are building, understand the pieces, and recognize how they all connect to the glorious life you choose to manifest.

Thrive Principle: Home is Within You

Your life is not something to finish or perfect. It's something to care for, shape, and return to. Build it with truth. Strengthen it with love. Repair it with grace.

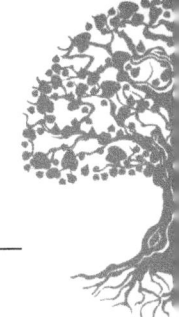

CHAPTER FIVE

Breaking Ground

The Willingness to Start

*B*reaking ground is the quiet, decisive moment when a vacant plot of land becomes a promise for *more*. That distinctive moment is more than just the act of driving a shovel into the soil. It is the pivotal moment when an idea transitions from paper blueprints to a *tangible reality*. When the surveyor stakes the land and plots the lines, you cross an invisible threshold that becomes the bridge from possibility to certainty, changing your attention from what *might* be to what *will* be. This is when a plan for constructing something meaningful becomes definitive. It is the stage known as *breaking ground*, both figuratively inside ourselves and physically in our lives.

Before that moment, the plans for such a structure may have sat folded on a table. The dream might have lived quietly in the mind, *waiting*. But once the shovel first cuts into the dirt, the dream unfolds. The work begins. What was beneath the surface now starts to rise. You stop worrying about what could potentially occur and start contemplating *what is about to happen*.

Great structures have emerged from such a decision to begin. The moment we transition from planning to building, we honour our desires through action rather than intention, and that is when resilience takes root. *We push past the old and welcome something new.*

Breaking ground in life follows the same rhythm. Drawing up ideas for change, exploring what feels possible, and slowly building the courage to begin can take months or even years. You may not notice it, but beneath the surface, something in you is *shifting.*

It can take months or even years to conjure up ideas for change, consider what is feasible, and build the courage to begin. We often need time to determine what is best and allow our inner fortitude to move us from where we are to what we *can* create. Like a tiny hermit crab vacating one home for the next, leaving itself exposed and vulnerable, we too must go from where we are to the next phase by *breaking ground* toward the new.

Trusting the Process

Before this phase begins, it often feels like nothing is happening. But that quiet season matters. Clearing land, preparing the soil, and making space are all part of the process. Progress may not be obvious right away, but it *is happening.* Bit by bit, the transformation is building inside.

Then, every step forward becomes concrete evidence that we are making progress. As we build a solid foundation, we rely on what lies beneath. Building resilience begins at this stage, which involves the decision to *break ground* where nothing existed before. It starts the moment you say *yes,* move the first clump of debris, and start doing the hard, internal work. This process is crucial in both life and whenever we want to build something.

Like a house, our lives need strong foundations. A lasting structure for our lives requires routines that keep us steady, values that hold us rooted, and relationships that help us through tough times. *Strong routines* keep us grounded. *Values* root us in purpose. *Relationships* support us through every kind of weather. These principles shape your life and values. A life that lasts is built on what is solid. These are the unseen layers that hold us steady when everything above the surface starts to shake.

We do not always notice the small disruptions. Yet, they occur and have an impact. Each person must decide to start anew, show up for themselves, and persevere even when things seem uncertain.

I have learned that a well-built home is not made for sunny days alone. It is made to survive rain, storms, and long winters. The same is true of our lives. Resilience is not a feeling we wait for. It is a stature we build slowly, intentionally, and often without applause. We build it through consistency, deliberate action, and showing up to *break ground* on what matters the most to us.

Resilience Markers for Breaking Ground

When we think of *breaking ground,* we often picture the dramatic first stroke of a shovel, but the real work begins long before that: in the quiet decisions, the sleepless nights, and the *"just one more try"* moments. These are the markers of resilience, the points when we choose not to surrender, when we stake our claim on possibility despite what the world tells us.

My father showed me these qualities throughout his life and confessed that his foundation, his belief in himself, stemmed from the moment he chose to *break ground* and be more than what the world told him was his plight.

If you asked him yourself, he would share that he was born into hard times and even harder choices. He did not discuss resilience the way we do today; instead, he lived it. My father never expected life to be easy. He expected to meet it through effort. He faced hardship without complaint and did what had to be done, even when the work was difficult.

Dad's strength was quiet and steady. He stood firm in who he was. Criticism never rattled him because he knew what he believed. There was a calmness in him that came from living his values and trusting his own path.

He was born in the early days of the Great Depression and learned resilience at a young age as a survival instinct. He witnessed his family sometimes moving homes in the dead of night to avoid unpaid rent.

Jobs were scarce, and his father, a gambler and bootlegger, was often absent. Even as the youngest son, Dad stepped up. He delivered papers and medicine on his bike and worked wherever he could to keep his family fed and sheltered.

When his father died, Dad was still a teenager, yet the weight of caring for his mother, siblings, and extended family fell on his shoulders. He accepted it with dignity. He showed up with practical advice, a steady hand, and a sense of humour that could lift even the heaviest day.

His past shaped his purpose. He found strength in doing the 'right' thing and never needed attention. He simply wanted results. He survived on mustard and ketchup sandwiches and only let that experience make him *more* determined. He started as a plumber, then became a builder, and finally a developer. He fixed homes and built entire neighbourhoods, creating *something lasting out of nothing.*

Building Good

Dad's goals were simple: *build a good life, raise a strong family,* and, if possible, *work together with the people you love.* He didn't expect someone else to solve his problems. He figured things out. He made it work. He never saw failure as something to fear. What he feared was not trying at all. He believed setbacks were part of the deal and that persistence was the only way forward.

I was forever watching him. He served not only as a father but also as a builder of a better life. His resilience shaped mine. His calm became my compass. I didn't understand his conviction and tenacity back then, but I felt it. And I carry it now. It serves as a reminder that the choice to become the best version of yourself isn't a matter of loudness. It is a quiet strength that stays with you when everything else feels like too much.

Dad persisted because he overcame doubt, trusted the invisible, was deeply spiritual, and believed in the efficacy of prayer. He made a silent vow to himself that he would be a success story, filled with hope, patience, and perseverance. His decisions would challenge conventional norms, combat stigma, and maintain his unwavering faith.

The most resilient people are those who have faced real burdens and troubles and persevered with relentless optimism. They persist in making progress, even when life's challenges continue to mount.

What I most admired about Dad was that he had become tired of merely scraping by. He decided that poverty would no longer define his life, and he faced every obstacle with double the determination. *His business dreams were his escape plan.* Looking back now, I realize *breaking ground* wasn't something Dad did once when he started a new project; he did it *every single day.* Dad's ability to break new ground in his life, day after day, stays with me. Whenever progress appeared unattainable and life appeared set to descend, he would awaken and choose resilience once more. On some days, he barely made progress, yet he never gave up. Every time he faced a problem, he chose to stick with it. Each time life hit him hard, he rose early to resume his work. Every time someone said he couldn't, he stayed steady and let the ground beneath him shake, and his foundation remained intact.

I have certainly followed in his footsteps. My life has had its moments of disruption, met with quiet decisions to start again when no one was watching. The most important shifts often begin without fanfare. I have seen how the seeds of change move in silence. But over time, what mattered was how I rose and decided to try again. I have broken ground, not with tools, but with truth. I have cleared a space in my life for something stronger, steadier, and more meaningful. The process has been slow, but the progress has been real, built on the resilience he showed me how to construct.

My father's legacy is the very ground I stand on. It is the reason I *keep* building. *Every* value he lived. *Every* lesson he taught. *Every* quiet act of strength. All of it lives on in the way he put the shovel in the dirt, broke ground, and declared what he knew: that he was worthwhile.

The Strength Patterns for Breaking Ground

Breaking ground means more than beginning. It means showing up when the ground beneath you feels uncertain. It means trusting that small actions matter. When you clear space in your life for something new, you begin to build strength.

Every strong structure is built on patterns that repeat and reinforce its design. The same is true in our lives. *Strength patterns* are the internal cadences and external habits that help us thrive through pressure and uncertainty. They are not complicated, often private, rooted in core beliefs, and built on small actions that compound over time. These patterns don't just help us survive hard times; they position us to grow stronger in the face of them.

Here are the top foundational patterns that help you *break ground* for a resilient life, grounded in purpose, and shaped by conscious choice.

- **Choose action over waiting.** You may carry a dream inside your mind, but the work begins when you step out of the planning stage and into the doing. The foundation of your growth is not built on vision boards or wishful thinking. *The foundation is established with the first cut of the shovel.*
- **Build a routine into your life.** A strong life does not rely on dramatic, exhausting efforts. It relies on repetition. The person who shows up when no one is watching is the one who builds something that lasts. *Let your values become habits. Let your commitments become rhythms. When your life rises from a quiet daily devotion, the storms will come, and you will remain standing.*
- **Root yourself in purpose.** When you know the 'why' behind your building, you withstand the pressure of 'how' and 'when.' Let your goals reflect who you are, not what others *expect* you to become. *Let the architecture of your life rise and stem from your truth, not your fear.*

- **Turn obstacles into design lessons.** A crack in the wall is not just damage. It is a teacher. A delay is not a failure. It is an opportunity. By embracing curiosity instead of moments of panic, you cultivate both wisdom and structure. *Strength grows when you face what needs repair and choose to rebuild intentionally.*

- **Understand that all progress is meaningful.** The land you cleared today may look empty. The foundation you laid may seem invisible. But underneath, roots are spreading. The beams are set. The deep work is happening. Trust that the unseen is as real as the visible. *Your strength is formed in those silent spaces.*

Remember that *breaking ground* is not a one-time event; *it is a way of living.* When you break ground, you *do not stop.*

You continue.

You *refine.* You *expand.*

Your life becomes an ongoing project, fueling your heart, skill, and faith.

As you look around and wish for more, ask yourself, "*What ground can I stand on? What plateau can I reach,* and *what do I need to break free from what has been holding me back?*" The day I stepped out of the women's shelter marked the beginning of my journey to explore new territory in every aspect of my life. I gave myself permission to start again because now I had the permit to rebuild. I was feeling sad and down, and I *knew* something had to change, because I couldn't keep living my life the way I was any longer.

Resilience is more than just enduring; for me, it was daring to abandon the unhealthy foundation I was never meant to stand on. Old fears, loyalties, and others' walls are the hardest soil to break. No one can grant you permission to start over and start fresh; therefore, you must grant it to yourself. Stepping upon fresh soil celebrates the finest version of yourself.

We all hold the tools to rebuild, repair, and rise. Knowing this, I broke free from the old. My future was uncertain, yet my life felt like a blank canvas. I was now an artist, ready for fresh watercolours and an entirely new blueprint.

Like me, you may face a new beginning or a challenging restart. Like me, you have the opportunity to use that experience as a catalyst to break new ground in creating the life you envision for yourself. Use the idea of digging in, moving dirt, and saying yes to what's next as an igniter for something wonderful. My dad always said, *"It won't happen if you don't start. It won't be successful if you don't give it all you've got."*

You were meant to thrive, and taking this first step marks the true beginning of your journey.

Thrive Principle: Breaking Ground

Breaking ground is the very point where your true shape and intention begin to reveal themselves. With excavation and construction underway, you commit. You stop wondering. You begin to build the very life you desire next.

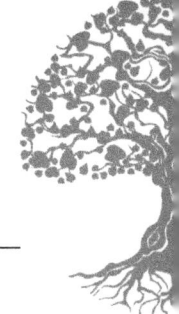

CHAPTER SIX

Foundation of Strength

We Get What We Build

Life doesn't just challenge us. *It tests our structure.* It shakes our certainty, rattles the floorboards of resolve, and exposes hidden cracks we didn't know were there. In these moments, it becomes clear that strength isn't just about standing tall. It's about what holds us together when everything around us threatens to fall apart. True resilience lies at the core, the root, and the *foundation of our life.*

Like a well-built house, a strong life needs a stable base. Without it, walls shift, doors stick, and everything above starts to falter. But with the right foundation of values, relationships, and personal practices, you can withstand just about anything.

Life tests us by shaking the structures we build, tearing down the walls of confidence, and whittling away at the doorways toward change. We don't always see it coming. But when the wind picks up and the ground shifts beneath our feet, it becomes clear very quickly whether what we've built can hold.

Just as a well-built house distributes its weight evenly to avoid sinking or shifting, people also need a foundation that stabilizes them when life grows heavy. Habits, commitments, and routines act like footholds to support our lives. When everything else falters, *that base keeps us upright and safe.*

People don't build foundations in moments of ease. They're laid down in hardship, in the weight-bearing seasons, the pressure points, and the decisions no one sees. These are the markers of *real* resilience within the foundational joints. They're *not* flashy or celebrated, but they are essential for overall structural success. A strong foundation will endure for many generations. Add solid principles, beliefs, habits, and genuine relationships, and you have formed the base of resilience and stability in life.

Now that you have broken ground, your next focus is on the foundations you build. This includes *your values, the routines you stick to when no one is watching, and the relationships you invest in, even if it costs you.* When you do this *fundamental* structural work, you are able to stand firm through countless seasons of uncertainty. Establishing a foundation gives you the ability to grow instead of simply existing. Most importantly, a strong foundation turns what could have been usable into the winning architecture of your life.

Putting in the Work

I have found that the foundation stage isn't the most popular. When I was rebuilding my life, I accepted that the process would be slow, steady, and largely invisible to the outside world. My first commitment was to the foundation. I began my activities early in the morning when the only individual I was accountable to was myself. I had to make decisions that would benefit not just my life but the *future I wanted to create*. I insisted on setting necessary boundaries even when they were inconvenient. Rebuilding my foundation was not a moment most people celebrate, but it was the one I could rely on to ensure stability.

What you lay down in your foundation will become the strength your future stands on. *Your foundation is the very thing you will come back to time and time again.*

When you feel yourself wobbling in life, a firm foundation becomes a guide, a strength, and a safe space. It reminds you of your values, why you're doing it, and what you won't compromise on.

After my upheaval, building a new life for me meant becoming the architect of my own inner circle and life. While reassembling my circumstances, I used the *foundation* I'd built to choose acquaintances more consciously, making sure they aligned with my values in every relationship going forward. I deliberately took more time to define what healthy relationships looked like, including things like mutual respect and honest communication.

These clear standards became my non-negotiable code and the structural footing I used to screen each new acquaintance. I finally developed the ability to trust my instincts, recognizing the subtle warning signs I had previously dismissed or ignored. I noticed early warning signs I had overlooked and communicated when boundaries were crossed. My unshakeable self-respect supported the most important structure I was building: a new life. That's a powerful combination. My focus on my personal code and the rules I had set for myself grounded me in a metaphor of stability and resilience.

As you advance in your life, you need a solid and predictable foundation you can hold yourself to. Your choices about who to spend time with, what opportunities to accept, and when to say *yes* are all determined by the foundation you build in moments of clarity and intention, not in moments of chaos or pressure. When life tests you, that foundation, reflecting your values, will help you navigate uncertainty.

Resilience Markers for the Foundation of Strength

A resilient life doesn't ignore the foundation phase. It prepares for it. It studies, learns, plans, and proceeds accordingly. Every time you show up, hold steady, or get back up, you're reinforcing a *powerful* foundation that will carry you through whatever comes next.

The fundamental challenge in 'rising up' is attempting to use a broken foundation to lift a heavy burden. The process of rebuilding requires focusing intently on the fundamental and core elements holding you together and strengthening your base.

For our family, that ever-present, unshakeable foundation was Dad. His resilience wasn't a performance. It was his way of being. He was the anchor, the steady base holding everything upright when the world grew unsteady. He used his pain as building blocks to strengthen himself, and he turned his grit into gratitude to better his self-worth. No matter the difficult moment he was facing, Dad relied on his foundational resilience and kept showing up. He didn't need comfort. He needed a purpose. Every hardship became part of the cement he was forming for a life he *believed in.*

My father's foundation wasn't perfect. It was poured over unstable ground: constant moves, strict rules, and a life full of obstacles. However, when he found his vocation in plumbing, something clicked. Learning a trade gave him purpose. It awakened the businessman within, and he became a man of sharp intellect and unstoppable ambition. He started small. *Brick by brick.* Bit by bit. Determined to create something of his own. What began as a desperate search for any paying job became something much bigger, the foundation of his beliefs.

People Give Us Strength

I remember a story about Dad when he landed an apprenticeship with the most feared plumber in town, Frank McGrath. Frank was known for being hard-nosed and relentless. Everyone called him *"Old Man McGrath,"* and when he gave you a job, you didn't ask questions. You just had to work.

For reasons known only to McGrath, he seemed to have a grudge against Dad. He assigned the hardest, dirtiest jobs imaginable to Dad and Robbie, who was my father's best friend at the time. These were the jobs that *no one else would touch.*

Dad loved recalling the time when Old Man McGrath ordered them to empty a full, rancid septic tank. *By hand.* Bucket by bucket. Inside the tank, in the middle of summer, dealing with the unbearable stench, Dad passed the pails up to Robbie, with the contents spilling onto his face, hair, and clothes. Even so, he didn't quit. He needed the work, the paycheck. So he did the job, start to finish.

Another gruelling job was at the local church. He was tasked with hauling a heavy, cast-iron radiator weighing over one hundred pounds up three flights of stairs. Old Man McGrath expected him to give up. But he didn't quit. Step by gruelling step, he and Robbie carried that beast to the very top. *No* shortcuts. *No* complaints.

Then there was a dangerous and unbearable boiler job. It involved crawling into a dark, suffocating, hot metal box filled with toxic fumes while scraping and sealing the filthy walls by hand. Most people would have walked away; *Dad pushed through.*

He often told me *these weren't just tests of strength; they were tests of character. Of resolve. Of grit.* Dad always said those jobs shaped him. They toughened him, taught him to endure, and, ironically, prepared him for future hardship.

Dad's strength wasn't just physical. It was emotional. He didn't just push through difficult things; he believed wholeheartedly in the possibility that something better was waiting on the other side. He had a deep, unwavering faith in himself and his future.

Even in love, Dad was bold. When Mom was engaged to someone else, someone her parents adored, Dad showed up at their engagement brunch uninvited, shouting through the front door, "Come with me, Betty! I can give you a better life." And she did. *She got up, grabbed her coat, and walked out.*

That's the man he was. Not polished, not always proper, but real, passionate, and determined. Unwilling to sit on the sidelines. That was his foundation, the person he built: honest, real, and completely authentic.

Through it all, Dad remained steady. He built his resilience not through easy wins but through a solid foundation he committed to, regardless of the challenges he faced. He built that foundation on persistence, self-belief, and a willingness to start over, regardless of the difficulties of the previous day. His foundation wasn't overbearing. It was true and consistent. It defined the resilience that we all need to live the life we want.

Strength Patterns for the Foundation of Strength

Strength doesn't just show up; it gets shaped, layer by layer, through the choices we make and the standards we keep. Once the foundation is poured, what follows are the structural patterns that reinforce it every single day. These aren't grand gestures. They're the subtle, often invisible actions that create consistency, form identity, and stabilize everything else.

Foundational resilience is shaped by patterns and deliberate choices repeated over time. These are the essential practices that allow you to endure hardships and emerge stronger.

Here are six key patterns that help build a foundation strong enough to hold your life steady:

- **Ground your life in your values.** The deeper your values (honesty, discipline, compassion, perseverance), the stronger your structure. When everything else feels uncertain, these principles become your inner scaffolding, reminding you who you are *and keeping you rooted in what matters.*
- **Let hardship teach you.** A tough situation doesn't mean you've failed. It means you're being shaped. Treat your setbacks like blueprints: study them, learn from them, and let them inform what you build next. *That's how you turn challenges into cornerstones.*
- **Build daily habits that reinforce stability.** Strength is not built in dramatic moments. It's built into routines. Wake up early. Do the work. Keep your word. Honour your commitments. These habits, practiced consistently, *lay the bricks of a dependable life.*
- **Surround yourself with people who reinforce your structure.** The people closest to you either strengthen your foundation or shake it. Choose those who see your worth, believe in your blueprint, and *are willing to get their hands dirty beside you when life gets messy.*

- **Hold steady through discomfort.** Real strength doesn't rush or panic. It holds. When life tests your patience, your timing, or your sense of progress, trust your groundwork. Trust what you've built. Not every storm requires a response. Sometimes, strength is found in *staying still and letting the winds pass.*

- **Practice daily consistency.** Resilience is built long before a crisis. It is cultivated through your daily routine, your interactions with others, and your commitment to following through. Repetition matters. Steadiness matters. *Set a steady pace that holds even when things fall apart.*

The Foundation That Holds Us

A foundation of strength and resilience keeps us standing when life tries to knock us down.

My father laid the groundwork for my life, providing the base upon which everything else rests. His core values serve as bedrock principles I can always count on: *honesty, kindness, discipline, healthy routines,* and *inner calm.* These are not just inherited qualities. They are coping strategies that have guided my decisions, parenting, career, *and* relationships.

Watching Dad build his foundation taught me that resilience isn't inherited; it's constructed. I didn't automatically gain his strength just because I was his daughter. I had to learn how to pour my own foundation, using the blueprints he showed me, but doing the work myself. These are the patterns I've discovered, both from his example and from rebuilding my own life.

Storms may come to everyone, but they cannot erase our identity. When we root our foundations in resourceful habits, strong convictions, and inner knowing, little feels uncertain. The foundations we build aren't always about reaching success. They're about forging a legacy that helps us thrive and prosper. The foundations we construct become the foundations others rely on. This is how we support ourselves and future generations.

The Wisdom of the Brick

I encourage you to lay a sound foundation and focus on it. Stories like *The Three Little Pigs* teach us this even as children. We all remember how the pigs who rushed the process, building with straw and sticks, saw their homes collapse the moment the wind picked up. However, the pig who took the time to build with bricks succeeded. His house stood strong. That tale may seem simple, but the truth inside it is profound. If you build your life on quick fixes, shortcuts, or popular trends rather than truth, it will not withstand pressure.

As we enter adulthood, we realize that problems don't just appear as wolves at the door. They show up as job loss, heartbreak, illness, rejection, or uncertainty. In those moments, the foundation you've built, *the carefully placed bricks*, holds greater significance than anything else. That's why we must build intentionally, with a resilience that anchors us and with values that hold us up.

I encourage you to look at your foundation and see where you can shore it up. Maybe it needs a revamp, an update, or even a complete overhaul. Regardless of its current condition, give your foundation attention, care, and focused effort. I once heard a person say, "*Nothing happens if nothing happens.*" Take your time to ensure your foundation is one you believe in and trust one hundred percent.

Thrive Principal: Foundation of Strength

Your life can only rise as high as your foundation is deep.
When you build from a place of strength, shaped by values and reinforced by resilience, you won't need to fear the storm. You'll simply know you were built to stand.

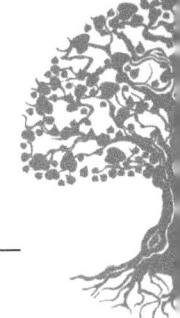

CHAPTER SEVEN

Framing the Structure

What Holds You Steady in Life

The foundation in our lives may bear the weight of what we experience, but it is the *framework* we build that helps give everything else its support.

Framing is the stage in your development where the *structure* you design becomes vitally important to your future happiness. Framing is what makes your life more than a shell or a box. It defines the space you truly need, creates the openings and doorways you dream of, and provides the structural support you need to enjoy. In this phase, you start to see the tangible *stability* of what you are aiming for.

In life, the framing stage is when your results become visible through your conscious choices *and* actions. This is the point when your efforts start to take shape, because you are finally ready foundationally. Framing your life *well* means establishing boundaries, routines, and standards that keep you steady when *things around you shift*. The frame you build today will ultimately determine how much more your life can carry later on.

As a child, I learned that when a builder frames a house, each beam connects seamlessly to another to ensure every board has a purpose, and when one is off, the whole structure feels the strain. The same is true in our lives. When we don't align our actions with our values or clearly define our boundaries, life becomes unstable. But when each element connects with intention and clarity, balance appears. The structure can carry more load, and its stability feels intact.

I am the first to say that framing your life isn't about rushing. It is about *attuning to and finding alignment*. It is about connecting *who* you are with *how* you choose to live. The framework you create is meant to support your dreams, ideas, and aspirations. This structural commitment is what shapes your conviction to persevere, strengthens your resolve, and fine-tunes your attitude toward the world.

The Erosion of the Foundation

Before I arrived at the women's shelter, my life was like a house falling apart. The structural damage didn't happen overnight; it built up slowly, year after year. I had ignored the cracks, the small warnings, and the quiet signs that something was profoundly wrong. By the time the walls finally gave way, I realized the slow, quiet erosion did the most harm. My foundational layers had eroded silently, like water damage behind a wall.

Most women don't leave a marriage over a single argument, and *I was no different.* It was the accumulation of pain, unmet needs, and disconnection over time that finally broke something vital inside. I'd spent so long ignoring the creaks and the warning signs that when my own walls finally gave way, *I had nothing solid left to stand on.* Pain is an important and deeply human emotion, and, *yes,* it's almost always more layered than just *one* cause.

The Intentional Framework

Framing your life according to your vision *awakens your potential and unveils your purpose.* Any structure can be beautiful, but without a solid frame, it cannot withstand pressure. Similarly, a person may appear confident or successful, but without internal structure, everything eventually begins to falter under the weight of expectations. A job can appear ideal, but without proper framing, it can quickly become hectic and chaotic.

Framing your life intentionally means making deliberate choices that ensure a stable future. If you focus on the framework, you'll honour the structures it supports.

Building Your Supportive Structure

For most people, how they frame their lives often determines how they handle pressure and stress. A strong frame distributes challenges evenly, keeping everything true to prevent collapse.

It's the frame that allows us to overcome, expand, grow, and thrive in new opportunities. When we build upon those qualities, *our frame can withstand almost anything.*

In practical terms, your framing should consist of daily habits, consistent routines, and clear boundaries. This is the structure that holds everything up, and it must be built with intent. To construct this supportive frame, focus on these elements:

- **Establishing daily habits and consistent routines** and setting clear, non-negotiable boundaries provides internal stability and defines and protects your space.
- **Choose your supporters wisely** and focus on relationships that fully support you. This ensures your external connections reinforce your structure too.
- **Develop your internal practices** that remind you of who you are, whether it's journaling, vision boarding, intentional self-talk, or mirror work. This strengthens your inner resolve.

Your only job now is to focus on *nurturing your own framework* rather than expending energy holding up someone else's crumbling structure.

When life feels heavy, you don't have to carry everything alone; *you distribute the pressure across the whole structure of the framework you have built.* This is when assurance and resilience come into play.

We often imagine resilience as simply bracing for hardship, but it is far more than that. It is the ability to expand, widen, and remain grounded. Joy, love, and new opportunities require such a foundational framework to be present and to increase. The structure you establish allows your evolution and potential broadening to take place. It houses your growth and provides you with the space you need to become more than you first believed.

You Are Your Framework

In the spirit of your structural transformation, I invite you to take a moment now to reflect on the framework of your life. *Where do you feel solid, steady, and supported? What aspects of your life feel unstable, strained, or stretched too thin?*

These aren't questions we're often taught to ask ourselves. We're expected to instinctively know our structure, or worse, to rebuild it only *after* everything has come crashing in. Not knowing these answers proves exactly why working on your framework matters. Your frame influences how you carry stress, receive love, navigate change, and show up when life feels overwhelming.

So, ask yourself, *who is standing beside you, helping you hold the weight? What practices have helped you stay upright?* Your answers to these questions will indicate what is missing and what requires your immediate attention. The framework you create for yourself, whether consciously or unconsciously, will inevitably shape the quality of your life. How you define that life, whether through success, fulfillment, or resilience, will always reflect the integrity of the structure you build toward having a thriving life and existence.

Resilience Markers for
Framing the Structure

For most of us, the framing stage is when resilience becomes most visible. It is where values meet boundaries and dreams meet discipline. Framing teaches us that *resilience is not built from rigidity but from a flexibility that moves and breathes within its shape.*

Resilience shows up when *you* keep showing up. It grows stronger each time you choose patience over panic, trust over fear, and *consistency over complexity.*

When you ensure your frame is built on integrity, you are no longer at the mercy of anyone else. You determine what holds you steady, and that is something no one else can break. My father understood this concept, though he never put it in these words. His life was framed by action, by showing up, and by building something he knew was formidable. He used resilience not as a way to be reactive, but to stay level. He prided himself on being structurally sound and foundationally steady.

To my Dad, framing was both literal and symbolic. He often said that a builder's true skill shows up when the walls go up because that is when precision matters. He believed that if you built the frame right, everything else could be adjusted, repaired, or replaced. But if the frame was crooked, the whole infrastructure would eventually show it.

Dad's ethics taught me that what you build in yourself matters just as much as what you build in the world. He framed his life around responsibility and the unshakeable bond between hard work and acts of service. He structured his family life around leading by example, lots of laughter, and showing love. When I think of his foundation, I see it in his character, the choices he made, and the stability he offered to everyone around him.

He possessed the ability to manage rejection, disappointment, and failure without ever losing his core values and focus. Whether it was a business setback or a personal loss, he would say, "*If the frame is good, you can fix the rest.*" Those words have constantly stayed with me. They remind me that building resilience is not about avoiding problems. It involves building a structure within yourself that can take a hit and still stand straight.

I think about how his business evolved, from plumbing to home building to real estate development. It began with a simple idea shaped by a relentless work ethic to build proper structures and scalable frameworks. He often said he was not just building homes; he was building something that could grow into something more. His firm conviction, not ambition, constructed his framework.

Dad's business began small but eventually employed hundreds of plumbers stretching across numerous regions. What struck me most was not the deals he made but the resilience it took for him to keep showing up. He knocked on doors again and again, facing rejection with calm persistence. Homeowners refused his services. Doors were often slammed in his face. Many would have given up. He did not. *Why?* Because he built a foundation that made him resilient.

Dad did not teach me lessons with grandiose speeches. He taught with presence, with doing, and with *always* showing up.

I have built my life on the framework Dad handed me. Despite their often subtle and understated nature, his actions consistently brimmed with purpose and significance. While I walked his job sites and sorted plumbing parts, I was learning more than how to build houses. I was learning how to build myself. I noticed that commitment to oneself is not optional, but always shows up. I practiced the habits he lived: being consistent, keeping my word, and tending to the small things with genuine care. I respected the importance of this framework, even when I felt deeply shaken. I chose to reinforce my structure even when no one noticed.

Now, I stand on ground that feels solid and true. And I carry forward a legacy of resilience, not as an idea but as a framework for thriving in all that I do. I share this because I want the same for you. A life built on a structure that gloriously works for you. A framework you can live by that *uplifts and inspires all that you do.*

Strength Patterns for Framing the Structure

I believe that resilience begins with showing up; it is shaped layer by layer through the choices we make and the standards we keep. Once the frame is in place, it reinforces our structural patterns and actions every day. These are not the patterns of grand gestures;

they are the subtle, consistent patterns that form your identity and stabilize everything you need.

Like a well-framed house, a resilient life depends on structural repetition. What you reinforce every day becomes what carries you when life demands more.

Here are four key patterns that help build a frame strong enough to hold your life steady:

- **Create boundaries that define your space.** Just as walls create rooms, boundaries define your emotional and mental space. They clearly show where you end and others begin. Healthy boundaries don't close you off; they give you structure. *They create the necessary space for peace, growth, and creativity.*
- **Strengthen your framework through repetition.** A strong structure depends on repeated patterns that reinforce beliefs. Your habits do the same. Keep showing up, doing the work, and following through. *Every act of follow-through tightens your frame and increases your stability in your beliefs about yourself.*
- **Reinforce your frame through connection.** Every structure needs crossbeams for support. In your life, the crossbeams represent your relationships. Build a support system that helps you carry the weight when life gets heavy. *Surround yourself with people who want to see you strong and secure.*
- **Be flexible under pressure.** A rigid frame cracks when the wind comes. A well-built one bends just enough to absorb the force. The same is true of your life. Adaptation is not weakness; it is wisdom. *The more flexible your perspective, the more enduring your resilience will be.*

The real beauty of framing your life is that the same framework that protects you can also allow you to expand and grow. A well-framed life enables inner growth because it is specifically designed to enhance and support your development. When your structure is sound, you can add new things, open new doors, and welcome more people around you without losing your stability.

Building a structure isn't about blocking things in; it's about opening up freedom. The more intentional your framework, the more space you create to live with clarity, peace, and purpose. The right framework doesn't confine you; it liberates you.

Your life deserves a frame that reflects your strength, values, and purpose. This isn't about closing yourself in. It's about creating a structure that holds you, supports your growth, and protects your peace. Like the framing of a house, your structure shapes the space where your dreams can live. You don't have to have it all figured out, but you *do* need to begin.

Start with what matters most: your values, your time, and your truth. Build your life around that. Every action, decision, and habit you choose, formulate it with intention because it will become the very support you need for the life you're creating.

This is your invitation to stop surviving and start formulating what you want. When you build a framework rooted in what's real and meaningful to you, resilience becomes part of your architecture. You're no longer just reacting to life, you're designing it. And when heartaches come, as they always do, your life won't fall apart. You will prevail because you took the time to frame it properly, the way **you** like.

Thrive Principle: Framing the Structure

A well-framed life is one that holds steady. When your structure is true, you can accomplish anything.

CHAPTER EIGHT

Opening Windows and Doors

Welcoming What Lies Ahead

Now that your foundation is solid and your framework is sound, *what's next?*

You begin to open.

You inhale, breathe in fresh air, let go of what's stale, and make room for *what's next*. When you allow yourself to open, you invite the world in. Too often, we mistakenly create barriers that keep us confined. We seal ourselves in, confusing protection for progress.

The windows and doors of your life are more than metaphors; they are intentionally allowing light, connection, growth, and transformation to enter. Life wasn't meant to stay boxed in, and neither were you.

My dad used to say, *"You don't really know what you've built until you open it up and let life happen inside it."* He believed homes and people should welcome the elements in: sunlight, fresh air, a knock at the door, and a laugh shared on the patio. All of that matters. He taught me that a house's strength wasn't only in how well it could withstand the elements, but in how openly it could receive joy and newness when the cloudy skies cleared. That perspective shaped how I perceived building resilience in my life: not as fortification, but as the flexibility needed to explore and see new vistas on my life's horizon. Our lives need intentional openings, just like a house needs windows and doors to be functional, breathable, and livable.

Opening windows is like allowing our souls to breathe. We bask in the radiance and bloom in the love, joy, and even disappointment that all arrive on our front step to help us expand.

In this openness, you begin to allow yourself to experience new possibilities. To adapt. To circulate.

In my life, I learned that creating space meant more than just quiet time or meditation. It involved releasing the need for control and certainty. It meant opening up emotionally, even when I was afraid. It meant allowing others to support me and being brave enough to stand in my truth without needing to shut everyone out.

Building those *resilience muscles* didn't only show me how to endure challenges and hardship; it transitioned me from merely surviving to actively *empowering myself.* They taught me how to welcome change. I learned to trust myself enough to remain open even when it was uncomfortable. I also learned to have faith in an uncertain future.

Leaving my old life behind and walking away with just two suitcases required all my strength. Yet, the real power wasn't in the walk itself. The true opening was the unfurling of my pain's release and the unlocking of the doors I had shut. That act of radical honesty finally empowered me to become the person I desired to be.

For a long time after leaving, I kept every door locked. Literally and figuratively. I didn't let people in. I didn't accept invitations. I didn't share my story. I convinced myself that staying closed was the same as staying safe. But isolation masquerading as protection is still isolation.

The turning point came quietly, as most important shifts do. A colleague invited me to a women's gathering, something I would have declined automatically. But that day, something in me whispered, "*What if you just say yes?*" So I went. Fearing exposure, judgment, or worse, pity, I stepped through that door.

Instead, I found women who had walked similar paths. They didn't need my defenses or explanations. They needed my presence. And in their presence, I experienced a gentle unfurling of something within me, akin to the opening of a window after a long winter.

I started sharing my story in small pieces. I didn't share the entire agonizing tale all at once, but instead, I shared candid moments. "*I've been where you are.*" "*I understand that fear.*" "*I rebuilt too.*" And every time I opened that door just a crack, life met me there with exactly what I needed. Life was not always comfortable, and at times, it presented challenges. Life didn't always bring answers, but it always brought growth.

Opening became my practice, not my prison. I learned to discern between healthy vulnerability and reckless exposure. I learned that closed doors kept out pain, but they also kept out light, connection, and hope.

That's when I truly understood: resilience isn't just about surviving with your walls up. It's about thriving with your heart open.

When you've established a robust foundation and framed your life with purpose, you realize your ability to handle any challenges that may arise and your readiness to venture beyond them.

Opening to Possibilities

As we move through life, we each face a choice: to stay tightly guarded or to let life in. And while boundaries are essential, windows still need glass and doors still need locks. We also need to be permeable. If nothing new can enter, *nothing new can grow either.*

Part of your resilience story is about developing wisdom, learning from others, and seeing what you didn't see before. It's about expanding your view, clarifying what's important, and considering what truly nourishes you. A well-built life has to have openings for light to get in. It has to carry thresholds so you can cross and return again. Such a place holds reverence for both the people you've welcomed in and the ones you've learned to release. This is the reason we want growth: *to become visible to ourselves and everyone else.*

You may be curious to know: *What doors in your life are still closed out of fear? What windows have been painted shut by old pain or assumptions? Where have you sealed off possibilities to avoid disappointment? And most importantly, are you ready to open them again?*

In opening more doors, you begin to see the opportunities that lie ahead. You find that peace matters more than approval, and *meaning outweighs accumulation.* Your priorities shift, and acceptance quietly takes root to bolster your resilience. The sharp edges of past struggles soften as your memory begins to favour the lessons you learned rather than the pain you endured.

Once you learn how to view life's challenges not only as interruptions but as invitations, your perspective expands to ask, *"What is this situation teaching me?"* That prompts your inner relationship to deepen. Experiences become more intense, and your awareness grows in enlightening ways. You discover that opening to what life offers isn't a sprint but a deliberate journey where intention shapes your full expression. At one point, you may have held the belief that success was determined by external factors, but you now realize that it's your internal contributions that truly matter.

When you open your inner doors and windows, you invite in a richer understanding of yourself. You activate exploration, connections, and ideas, and as a result, *you no longer fear the unknown.* You value what you've built because you see a life of opportunities, *not* limits.

Resilience Markers for Opening Doors and Windows

My father had a saying: *"If a door doesn't open, build another one."* He did not consider it a metaphor; rather, it was practical advice from a man who understood that people create pathways; they don't simply find them.

In his life, he created opportunities where none existed. Whether it was rebuilding after storms or expanding his business through sheer persistence, Dad didn't wait for permission to grow. He didn't seal himself off after rejection. *He knocked again.* Or better yet, *he framed a new entrance.*

I remember when he helped a fellow tradesman recover after Hurricane Hazel had devastated much of the region. The destruction created not just chaos but also opportunity because new homes were needed, new plumbing systems had to be installed, and builders had to step up. Rather than closing in and focusing on his own survival, Dad chose to open his resources, his time, and his wallet to help someone else. He believed that *what we give away always finds its way back.*

His resilience was a deep-seated willingness to keep his heart and hands open. He would say, *"People are the reason you keep the doors open. Otherwise, what are you building it all for?"* Those words stayed with me. They reminded me that strength is not about isolation. It's about integration. It's about letting life in, even when it might mess things up *a lot.*

My Dad didn't build homes to shut people out. He built them for shelter, connection, and as an opening. His hospitality, work ethic, and unwavering belief in human potential demonstrated his resilience.

Watching him navigate loss, disappointment, and uncertainty taught me that openness is a form of wisdom. He wasn't foolishly optimistic. He was intentionally receptive. And there's a big difference.

I've learned that resilience often looks like showing up again with your heart open, even after you've been hurt. It means trusting the strength of your structure enough to crack open a window or creak open a door, knowing you'll be okay, no matter what.

Discover the places in your life where you feel openness. Welcome others in and stand back to see what beauty unfolds.

Strength Patterns for Opening Doors and Windows

Many of us do not know how to 'open the curtains,' let alone the windows and doors. We have become a shut-out and shut-down society that no longer encourages such freedom as in my father's day. That is why this step is so vital and requires dedication and commitment.

If you dedicate yourself to one thing in life, it should be *yourself, your personal growth, and your inner light.*

Use the list below of *resilience markers* to guide you through this phase and make it a cherished one. Try each of these markers for a week to see how your life improves. A willing participant must support openness, which is a strength. Without structure, openness can become hectic. With structure, *it becomes growth.*

Here are the top *strength patterns* that help you open your life intentionally and meaningfully:

- **Let in the light.** Just as a window allows sunlight to brighten a room, you must allow truth and awareness to illuminate your life. Stop avoiding hard conversations, unresolved feelings, or your own unmet needs. Light makes things visible. *Visibility is what allows healing.*
- **Choose intentional entry points.** Not everything and everyone belongs in your life. Doors are meant to open with discretion. Establish your boundaries with clarity. You can be welcoming without being permissive. *You can be open without being exposed.*
- **Create emotional airflow.** A stagnant environment creates stress. So does emotional stagnation. Your life needs circulation: movement, refreshment, and release. *Make space for emotional processing. Talk. Write. Reflect. Allow your inner world to breathe.*
- **Build connection bridges.** Relationships are the walkways between isolated rooms in your life. Reach out. Ask for help. Offer help. Invite people in. *Isolation might feel safer in the short term, but connection is what sustains you long term.*

- **Be flexible to change.** A door opens in two directions. Sometimes you step out into the world, and sometimes the world comes to you. Either way, openness means being ready to adapt. *Change is not a threat; it's an invitation.*
- **Reopen after closing.** If you've shut yourself down because of past hurt, give yourself permission to try again. Reopening doesn't mean forgetting; it means healing enough to trust yourself. *Sometimes, the greatest resilience is found in your decision to begin again.*

Thrive Principle:
Opening Doors and Windows

A life that thrives knows when to open. You let people in. You welcome opportunities in. You let love, risk, and possibility move freely through your life. The more you allow in, the more you let life flow through you, not around you.

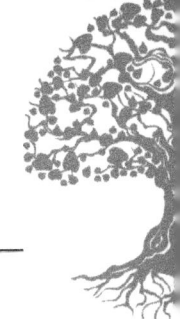

CHAPTER NINE

Reframing & Renewal

Shifting Perspective, Restoring Meaning

Until now, I've used the process of building a house as a metaphor for personal development you can undertake to help you *build* and *create* a more enjoyable life. Everyone can relate to this analogy, which emphasizes the fact that a house is never completely finished. *It unfolds. It breathes. It settles. It weathers storms and time.* And if you want it to last, you don't just build it once and then walk away. *You return to it. You restore it.* You repair the cracks before they widen and enlarge, and you reinforce what time and use have worn down.

The same applies to the life you're building and making right now.

You've broken ground, laid your foundation, framed your structure, and opened your doors. But without renewing what once was, even the strongest life begins to strain. Without the ability to reframe what you've experienced, even the most resilient spirit can get stuck in old patterns that no longer serve.

This is where reframing and renewal become essential maintenance, not optional extras. Not because something is broken, *but because growth requires us to see differently and reconnect to what truly matters.*

The Art of Reframing

Reframing is the gentle art of shifting perspectives to see new possibilities and renewal where there was once only exhaustion and depletion. It's choosing to view obstacles not as walls but as blueprints for something stronger. It's recognizing that how we see our circumstances shapes how we respond to them.

We often view life's challenges as problems to solve. But a builder has a different perspective. A builder views a crack in the wall as an opportunity to reinforce it. A delay is a chance to create better arrangements. A storm serves as a reminder to improve the structure next time.

Approaching life as a builder reshapes your mindset from victim to creator. The question changes from *"Why is this happening to me?"* to *"What can I make out of this?"* Each difficulty builds resilience, and each mistake serves as a design lesson or an invitation to improve the next layer with more care and understanding.

Reframing your life and reflecting on where it has brought you to right now is resilience in motion. This is the action you take when life's pressures, setbacks, or changes pull you off balance. Reframing allows for course correction and redirecting your energy wisely. It's the process of *pausing, assessing,* and *adjusting* so you can return to alignment with your true direction.

Reframing in Daily Life

I like to think of reframing as an act of self-awareness. It's a form of self-trust in which you take a moment to think, reassess, and adjust your course so you can proceed with greater inner calm and purpose rather than rushing. Reframing involves updating your trajectory guilt-free and letting go of things that no longer fit or serve you.

For many of us, reframing can be as simple as changing our morning routine, improving self-talk, or curating who we allocate our energy to. It's knowing when to accelerate and when to decelerate. Life moves with the seasons, and what worked last year may not work now. We need to keep recalibrating and rebalancing, because variety and change keep us renewed and refreshed. Each reframe you do incorporates lessons from what came before, creating something more thoughtfully constructed for the future.

I have seen how reframing requires honesty about our limits and creativity about our responses. Our shift in language changes everything. When we reframe exhaustion as information rather than failure, we respond with *wisdom* instead of shame. When we reframe rest as preparation rather than retreat, we give ourselves permission to truly restore, and when we shift our perspective from feeling inadequate to honouring what serves us, we practice genuine self-care and self-respect.

I have had to reframe my actions and decisions time and time again when I was annoyed by a friend, argued with my kids, or made decisions that were not conducive to my health. Each time, I used the experience to *reframe* my behaviour and *reset* my attitude. I didn't dwell on the negative; I immediately moved to reframing what I could improve.

I've learned that the most resilient people aren't those who never struggle. They're the ones who reframe struggle as *growth*. They see setbacks as setups for comebacks. They recognize that every challenge carries a *hidden gift* if we're willing to look for it as a lesson, not a hardship.

Once you learn how to view life's challenges not only as interruptions but as invitations, your reframing expands. You begin asking, *"What is this situation teaching me?"* That question prompts your inner relationship to deepen. Experiences become more intense, and your awareness grows in enlightening ways. And you look forward to a reframe to get you back on track.

Resilience Markers for Reframing & Renewal

Dad's influence and his evolving priorities taught me the value of reframing, reflection, reorientation, and remaining open to wisdom from every experience. Dad possessed a unique ability to discern when it was appropriate to pivot, adjust course, or relinquish something that was no longer fulfilling its intended purpose. That skill alone saved Dad enormous energy, allowing him to direct his efforts toward solving real issues rather than fighting shadows or worrying about what was outside his control. He conserved his energy by reframing *how* he saw challenges. Instead of being overwhelmed by what was wrong, he focused intently on what could be fixed.

Dad had a relentless drive for productivity and achievement. He treated his energy as if the supply were bottomless, until his unexpected heart attack shattered that illusion. As part of his recovery, his cardiologist prescribed a daily ritual: going home for lunch, resting, and taking a nap. This was a vital reframe for his life and a necessary renewal of the behaviours he needed to adjust.

Dad embodied reframing as a principle. After his heart attack, he could have seen the daily nap as a sign of decline or weakness. Instead, he reframed it as his secret weapon, his investment in longevity and sustained energy. He would say, *"I'm not slowing down. I'm pacing myself for the long race."*

That shift in perspective changed everything. *Rest, became intentional. Renewal became strategic.* And his life extended far beyond what anyone expected, not because he pushed harder, but because he learned to see differently.

Life demanded change, and Dad was able to maintain his workload and lifestyle by reframing his daily activities. His heart attack made one lesson unavoidable: *even the strongest among us cannot thrive on willpower alone.* But more importantly, how we frame what happens to us determines whether we grow from it or it diminishes us.

Over time, I, too, discovered that the unwillingness to reframe could impede growth. When I wasn't willing to face my problems, they only became more intense. When I reframed the importance of my problems, I shifted their impact on my life. Reframing gave me the ability to release with grace, a fresh perspective, and inner guidance. When I stopped and rebalanced what wasn't working, I learned to trust in both the wisdom of experience and the power to change.

Trusting my inner guidance helps me navigate through life's challenges and expectations. In moments of upheaval, when the world feels unmoored, internal knowing keeps me aligned. Key elements of reframing now include achieving success and feeling alive, being in tune, and being rooted in what truly matters. I often ask myself, "*What really matters most to me, and what do I want to grow and protect?*"

Reframing means adapting rather than avoiding. It means feeling free enough to welcome change and growth as life-enhancers, not punishments. I've learned that the most resilient people are those who overcome tiredness and struggle. They're the ones who recognize when they need to see differently and respond with intentional renewal. They reframe their relationship. They build meaning into their rhythm rather than waiting for life to feel meaningful on its own. They are able to be thankful in the face of adversity, and they look to renew their energy toward what will serve them best.

Strength Patterns for Reframing & Renewal

Reframing requires a decision. Renewal requires taking action.

Once you decide to reframe, the next step is renewal. By paying attention to your evolving self-awareness and following your inner guidance, you welcome a surge of fresh perspective that will renew your attitude.

A *strength pattern* for renewal teaches you to embrace your newfound wisdom by being curious, knowledgeable, daring, and open to stepping outside your comfort zone. Let your desire for renewal take you to places both figurative and literal. Treat yourself with kindness and compassion, and allow renewal to be a natural part of your passage through life.

As I had to step back into my life after walking out, I needed to *renew* many of the old thought patterns and limiting beliefs I had carried. I also had to set new patterns and take new actions to reinforce the renewal I wanted to take place. Managing my daily routine of wholesome living, healthful renewal, and sustainable self-care took time to integrate. For my life to unfold and thrive, I valued sleep, joy, relationships, and purpose. These were essential in my renewal phase. I intentionally cultivated them and made sure they were present in every aspect of my life.

Renewal is a journey many of us go on, and it is deeply personal and specific. What works for one person may not be ideal for the next. The key is recognizing it's a journey you must go on intentionally, yourself. Find what renewal means to you, and try many things to see what works and what doesn't. Remember that your renewal is vital, and by searching for it, *you will find it.* It won't come to you. You must discover and uncover it with purpose and desire.

Here are the essential patterns that help me reframe and renew my life intentionally:

- **Reframe challenges as invitations.** Focus on your goal, not your obstacle. Everyone perceives and responds to stressors differently. Your ability to reframe and renew reactionary patterns determines whether challenges will set you back or refine you. *That single shift transforms you from victim to victor.*
- **Practice gratitude as perspective medicine.** Gratitude and a clear sense of purpose are powerful sources of renewal in life. When we shift into gratitude, we reframe draining experiences by finding the hidden gifts or lessons they carry. Gratitude isn't about pretending everything is fine. *It's about finding what's real and good even when things are hard.*
- **Reconnect to your purpose regularly.** The soul needs meaning to sustain itself. Discover your life's purpose and feel in tune. Renew your passions, do what brings you joy, and see where you can give more than you receive. *Purpose provides the necessary fuel to keep you going and makes each day rewarding.*

- **Recalibrate without guilt.** Life moves with seasons, and what worked last year may not work now. Give yourself permission to adjust course. Ask, *"Is what I'm doing still working and serving me?"* Let go of outdated objectives no longer serving you. *Recalibrating means updating your direction without shame.*

- **Process emotions honestly and restore emotional energy.** Emotional energy is the current flowing through our relationships and our inner world. It powers patience, fuels creativity, and sustains resilience, but only when it's cared for with honesty, connection, and love. Your emotional energy depletes when conflicts go unresolved, emotions are suppressed, or relationships take without giving. It renews when you process feelings honestly, nurture mutual connections, and practice self-compassion and forgiveness. *Restoring emotional energy often means revisiting the past with a new perspective, making amends where possible, or reframing memories with gratitude and love for lessons learned.*

- **Cultivate relationships that energize you.** Developing sincere relationships that support you is essential. Prioritizing your most important relationships helps you feel supported, seen, and safe. All humans possess an innate need for connection, and to fully realize their potential, individuals must cultivate vitality, meaningful relationships, and a sense of purpose. Face people who drain you and then let them go without fear. A renewed mindset blends work and love without losing oneself. *Emotional energy grows through authentic, nourishing mutual connections* rather than depleting ones.

- **Give generously, and circulate your energy.** Your energy expands through movement and circulation. When you give generously from your strengths, share knowledge, or help others, you feel more energized. Think of your energy like muscle strength, which develops and grows through the right balance of challenge and recovery cycles. *Emotional energy flourishes when you acknowledge your feelings, cultivate relationships that nourish you, and let gratitude transform draining experiences into sources of renewal.*
- **Align your life with your values.** I thrive when my values align with how I live, whether through music, relationships, inner peace, or harmony. My family supported me in countless ways as I struggled to find balance. Dad championed kindness above all, and I strive to cultivate harmony so my spirit and heart can flow freely. *Building resilience, adaptability, endurance, and self-preservation requires addressing both immediate necessities and developing long-term strategies enabling us to truly flourish and thrive.*

Renewal is a process. *Remember that.* It takes time and effort and is meant to be slow and nurturing. The whole point of renewal is that it seeps in. It marinates. It unwinds. Rushing and pushing yourself have the opposite effect. Renewal is a practice. Renewal is not something you perform; it is a perspective you gain to allocate your priorities. Make your renewal a pleasant, enjoyable event so it becomes part of the fabric and legacy of your life.

When you reframe how you see your life and renew what gives it meaning, you don't just maintain what you've built; *you renew it and transform it.* You create the clarity, connection, and conviction to keep building something that truly matters.

Thrive Principle: Reframing & Renewal

The way you see your life shapes how you live it. When you reframe challenges as teachers, and renew your connection to meaning, you build a life that doesn't just endure but transforms through everything.

CHAPTER TEN

Rest & Repair

The Body's Blueprint for Healing

While writing this book, I often escaped to our family cottage. There, I nestled in the creative flow and felt the nostalgia of a place where so many family memories took root. I cherished the restoration and renewal those summers offered.

Yet, every summer had to come to an end. We took meticulous care to pack up the cottage, turn off the lights, cover the lawn furniture, shut down the utilities, and carefully close it up for the season. It was as if we were giving it a long, earned rest after extremely active months. We lovingly allowed the cottage to relax and restore until we returned the following spring.

The cycle of use, rest, activity, and restoration taught me something essential about how we're meant to live. Our bodies and minds, like the cottage, need seasons of intentional rest to settle, *be still,* and recover from the wear of joyful summers.

You cannot build without breaking down. You cannot grow without wearing down. And you cannot sustain what you've created without deliberate, intentional repair.

In construction, repair isn't failure. It's simply maintenance. It's proof that what you built is worth keeping, worth tending, and worth the care it takes to make it last. Cracks don't mean your foundation was poorly laid. They mean your house has been lived in, that it has served its purpose, endured challenges, weathered storms, and held weight.

Rest and repair are the unseen architects of resilience. They work quietly, often invisibly, rebuilding what daily life wears down. Without them, even your strongest efforts eventually suffer.

This chapter is about the restoration your body requires to not just survive but to *thrive*. It's about understanding that rest isn't passive. It's the most active form of self-preservation you have, the sacred closing-up of yourself so you can return truly renewed.

The Power of Rest

Many of us are caught in seven-day workweeks, juggling deadlines, commuting long hours, answering emails late at night, and feeling the constant pressure to keep achieving more. Even when we pause, our minds rarely switch off because we're constantly scrolling through news feeds, checking notifications, or mentally running through tomorrow's to-do list.

We often get stuck in a harmful cycle, convincing ourselves to prioritize exhaustion and convincing ourselves that constantly pushing harder is the only path to success. But this relentless drive carries a price, inevitably leading to burnout, fading health, and serious strain on our relationships. No matter how much we achieve, it still doesn't feel like enough.

Think about how often you tell yourself, "*I'll rest when the project is finished. I'll recharge after things calm down.*" Yet 'later' rarely seems to arrive... The truth is success built on constant depletion and exhaustion is fragile, and eventually cracks.

Rest as Resilience

We rarely connect rest with success, yet it's our deepest source of resilience, allowing us to gather strength, even in the midst of pressure. Our fast-paced lives command us to work faster, achieve more, and push harder. Taking time to repair the wear and tear on our minds and bodies is often considered a luxury we can't afford. We have forgotten that even the most sophisticated machines require regular downtime for maintenance, yet we expect our minds and bodies to run at peak capacity indefinitely.

The irony is striking: in our continuous quest for productivity, we often become less productive. In our relentless pursuit of *more*, we diminish our capacity to achieve anything truly meaningful. We mistake motion for progress, confusing the frantic spinning of our wheels with genuine forward momentum. But *what if rest isn't the opposite of success but rather the secret ingredient? What if the pause isn't where productivity dies, but where it goes to be reborn?*

Rest is not wasted time. *Repair is not a weakness.* They are the hidden engines of resilience, allowing you to keep showing up for your work, relationships, and health with a clear sense of purpose. Without rest, there is no real success. There may be movement and productivity, but without intentional, deliberate pauses for recovery, we're only pushing ourselves closer to the inevitable crash of exhaustion and depletion.

The Science of Repair

We often forget that our bodies are designed and wired to repair themselves, especially when we create the optimal conditions for true rest. The key to unlocking your built-in maintenance and repair system is intentional rest. Deep rest is an active process that allows your brain to clear waste, your muscles to rebuild, your immune system to strengthen, and your emotions to finally process and integrate.

Rest is your body's natural maintenance plan at work and is one of the most powerful investments you can make for sustaining long-term resilience. Rest and repair are active forms of restoration, encompassing far more than sleep alone. True rest engages your body's natural repair and maintenance systems:

The advantages of rest extend beyond just feeling rejuvenated. During restorative moments, your body shifts out of the sympathetic 'fight-or-flight' mode into the parasympathetic 'rest-and-digest' state. In this state, stress hormones like cortisol naturally decline, and your body activates repair systems that reduce inflammation, strengthen immunity, and promote optimal cellular regeneration.

When you rest, the fatigue-inducing chemicals, such as adenosine, that accumulate during wakefulness, finally clear from your system, naturally restoring your mental sharpness and focused attention that exhaustion has clouded. Even naps as short as twelve minutes can lower stress hormones, significantly reducing the energy drain caused by constant stress.

Types of Rest That Restore

True rest encompasses multiple dimensions, encompassing far more than sleep alone. Each rest type serves as a pathway back to balance and renewal. Biological maintenance comes in many forms, and understanding them helps you choose what you need most.

True rest is multifaceted. To genuinely recover, we need to address several dimensions:

- **Physical rest** allows our bodies to heal and strengthen. This includes sleep, naps, and simply lying down to let your muscles release tension and letting your cardiovascular system recalibrate without strain.

- **Mental rest** requires stepping away from constant problem-solving, decision-making, and information overload. Try meditation, engaging in repetitive activities like hiking, knitting, or gardening, or working silently without podcasts or social media. Your mind needs periods where it can simply exist without an agenda.

- **Emotional rest** occurs when you're with people who fully accept you and don't require you to manage their feelings. Occasionally, it's the profound relief of not having to be 'on,' whether you're alone or with people who provide genuine emotional safety and support, allowing you to simply be yourself without performance or pretence.

- **Sensory rest** means reducing stimulation from screens, noise, crowds, or intense environments. Your nervous system processes constant input even when you're not consciously aware of it. Quiet, dim, simple environments let your systems reset and renew.

Adequate rest strengthens our emotional immune system. Dad knew and understood this lesson well. When we rest, we handle stress better, react less to triggers, and respond more thoughtfully rather than impulsively. Rest creates the emotional space we need to process experiences, integrate difficult emotions, and maintain perspective during challenging times. Our emotional stability becomes the foundation for all other aspects of resilience.

Rest is a quiet repair that keeps us strong. In a world equating constant motion with worth, the art of true rest is both revolutionary and essential. Our culture's relentless emphasis on doing more, achieving more, and optimizing every moment has led to a collective forgetting of rest's profound power. We've been conditioned to view downtime as a wasted opportunity, yet it's precisely in the quiet moments that our deepest healing and repair occur.

Rest heals, cracks are mended, and strength is restored. Create repair conditions for yourself to protect your rest from our productivity culture. Rest is a biological necessity that builds your resilience and allows you to thrive. Make rest genuinely restorative by removing things that keep your system activated, like putting your phone in another room, choosing a calm environment, or setting boundaries around when you are available. Trust your body's repair timeline and treat rest as the foundation of your life. As my mom used to tell my dad, "*When you're properly rested, everything else becomes easier.*"

Our parents and grandparents often lived by regular daily patterns of work and pause, built around seasonal farming, restful Sundays, or simply gathering on porches at nightfall. They understood rest was a form of wisdom, rather than indulgence. Pauses and repair allowed them to conserve strength, foster genuine connection, and keep their perspective sharp. Reclaiming my parents' slower pace is an act of generational honour.

Quality rest prevents the need for crisis recovery. Regular restoration involves maintenance rather than emergency rigour. Resting and napping teach us about our actual needs. When we're constantly busy or stimulated, we lose touch with our body's signals, our emotional patterns, and what generally nourishes us.

Rest creates the quiet recovery, and space necessary to learn and hear our inner wisdom. The deepest repair happens when we stop trying to optimize rest and simply allow it. Our body knows how to heal when we provide it the space and safety to do so.

Deep rest reveals itself as the profound presence of renewal in your life. In sacred and intentional pauses, your brain clears and resets, your muscles repair and strengthen, your immune system reinforces its defence, and your emotions obtain space to settle and integrate.

Rest is an unseen repair crew working tirelessly while you breathe.

Resilience Markers for Rest & Repair

For Dad, physical restoration, laughter, recovery, and quality rest allowed his body to perform essential and critical maintenance work that could only happen during his downtime. When we sleep, our muscles repair microtears from daily activities, our immune system strengthens its defences, and our cardiovascular system recalibrates. Our growth hormone releases, cellular repair accelerates, and our body literally rebuilds and renews itself, becoming stronger than before.

For years, I believed Dad's energy was infinite. I watched my father embody relentless work, driving himself harder, faster, and longer. His unexpected heart attack shattered the illusion of his infinite energetic supply.

As part of his recovery, his cardiologist prescribed a non-negotiable, daily ritual: going home for lunch, resting, and taking a nap to bring his heart rate and blood pressure down before returning to work. Rest and repair were not luxuries for Dad. They became the cornerstones of a life capable of enduring hardships, fostering prosperity, and enabling us to transition from mere survival to thriving.

Taking time each day to rest became, for Dad, an investment in work yet to come. He learned to see rest as the foundation upon which all meaningful productivity is built. His heart attack made the lesson unavoidable: *even the strongest among us cannot thrive on willpower alone.* Energy is a resource, and resources must be replenished if we want to last.

By witnessing Dad's quick recovery and extended work life, I, too, became a strong believer in the power of even a short nap and the strength of silence. A brief rest supports heart health and circulation, lowering blood pressure and heart rate to give the cardiovascular system a micro-reset.

Strength of mind often begins with stillness. Dad would take a break during long, hard days and close his eyes for a few minutes of peace and quiet. To others, it appeared that Dad was napping, but he was rebuilding his focus and drawing fresh energy for the afternoon workday ahead. Dad found clarity and inner strength by paying attention to what his body needed.

When Dad was rested, the business and life problems that once felt overwhelming became far more manageable. Creative solutions emerged naturally, work felt less forced, and his relationships flowed more smoothly.

Whenever Dad faced a large business decision, he would always say, "*I want to sleep on it and wait twenty-four hours before making a final decision.*" His body's innate wisdom was at work, and it was one of the most strategic choices he could make to build resilience and sustain a life of purpose, impact, and genuine thriving.

Rest That Serves You

Napping offers powerful emotional and energetic benefits. Fatigue often erodes patience and emotional balance, but intentional rest restores our capacity to respond calmly, rather than react impulsively. Short, intentional naps act as mood stabilizers and energy boosters, replenishing reserves much like recharging a battery. Even a brief nap of ten to thirty minutes can refuel both your body and mind, support memory, sharpen problem-solving skills, and leave you more resilient for the rest of the day.

Think of a nap as your mind's filing system at work, sorting, archiving, and clearing space for fresh insights. Even a brief twenty-minute rest can sharpen your focus, boost your learning, and prepare you to absorb new ideas. During the reset, your brain acts like a lead architect, strengthening important memories, consolidating meaningful experiences into long-term storage, and sweeping away mental clutter. Think of the process as hitting 'save' on what matters and 'delete' on what doesn't. Cognitive renewal helps you think more clearly, make better decisions, and approach challenges with a fresh perspective.

Sleep consolidates memories, helping us retain learning and integrate new information with existing knowledge. As my mom always told me when I was studying for an exam, *"You can only study so much, so go to bed, get a good night's sleep, and your brain will remember your topics for the exam."*

My friends even nicknamed my sister and me the "Snore Sisters" because of our love for afternoon naps, and honestly, they might be onto something because naps fuel us with fresh energy, clear focus, and the spirit to tackle whatever comes next. A nap rejuvenates our minds and restores their structural integrity.

Similar to interval training in sports, alternating between exertion and recovery allows you to maintain a greater overall energy level than constant, unbroken efforts. Using naps effectively can be as simple as understanding the different types and choosing what your body needs most.

A power nap of ten to twenty minutes is best for a quick boost in alertness without grogginess. A longer nap of sixty to ninety minutes completes a full sleep cycle, enhancing creativity and memory. Even five to fifteen-minute rest breaks, whether lying down or deep breathing, helps your nervous system switch and restore balance.

Finally, rest can enhance creativity and problem-solving. During restful states, our brain's default mode network becomes active, generating revelations and interpretations. Many breakthrough solutions emerge during our walks, showers, or quiet moments of stillness when our minds can wander freely and make new associations. The paradox of rest is that *by doing less, we become capable of much more.*

Your body needs both pushes and pauses. The cycle of exertion and recovery fuels sustained energy, helping you perform at your best. Driving yourself nonstop only drains you, but when you build in recovery the way athletes do between sprints, you unlock more energy, more focus, and more strength than constant effort ever could. True endurance comes from the balance between action and restoration. We meet challenges with recovery and rest, which brings clarity, strong focus, and lasting resilience.

Strength Patterns for Rest & Repair

The most resilient people don't wait until they're burned out to rest. They schedule restoration before depletion sets in. They understand that rest isn't a retreat; *it's the foundation that makes all forward motion possible.*

Replenishing our reserves becomes an act of self-care. A short walk, a deep breath, and a brief retreat from noise can rekindle creativity and strengthen our resolve. The body thrives through both engagement and rest. Exertion awakens potential, while rest allows repair to settle in. Calm restoration and our ability to recover guide us back toward balance and equilibrium.

Every deliberate pause restores our capacity. Through stillness, our body repairs, our mind clears, and our strength returns. Quiet rest strengthens our ability to meet life with energy, clarity, and a resilient body.

Here are the essential patterns that help you build intentional rest and repair into your life:

- **Schedule rest proactively, not around your collapse.** Make rest a regular practice, not an emergency response. Your body repairs best when rest is consistent, not crisis-driven. Consider scheduling downtime during productive periods, rather than waiting until you are barely able to function. *Prevention is always easier than crisis recovery.*
- **Protect your rest from activation.** Rest only restores when it's truly protected. Put your phone in another room. Choose calm environments. Set clear boundaries around your availability. Eliminate the things that keep your system alert and activated. *Give your nervous system permission to fully let go.*
- **Align and match your resting activity with the specific dimension (mental, emotional, or physical) that needs replenishment.** Mental exhaustion needs mental rest and stepping away from decisions and problem-solving. Emotional depletion needs emotional rest: time with people who accept you for who you are, not for your performance.

Physical fatigue needs physical rest: actual sleep and stillness. Sensory overload needs sensory rest: quiet, dim, simple environments. *Identify depleted areas and restore them accordingly.*

- **Use strategic naps for renewal.** Experiment with naps. A power nap of ten to twenty minutes boosts quick alertness without grogginess. A longer nap of sixty to ninety minutes completes a full sleep cycle, enhancing creativity and memory. Even brief rest breaks of five to fifteen minutes, lying down, or deep breathing help your nervous system shift and restore balance. *Experiment to find what works for your body.*

- **Honour your body's repair timeline.** Your body has its own wisdom about healing. Trust the process. Don't rush recovery. Sleep consolidates memories, repairs tissues, balances hormones, and strengthens immunity. The deepest repair happens when we stop trying to optimize rest and simply allow it. *Let your body do what it was designed to do.*

- **Create daily repair rituals.** End your day with something that signals to your body it's safe to restore. Reading, meditation, journaling, or simply unplugging lets your body focus its energy toward repair rather than carrying stress into tomorrow. Small, consistent rituals compound into major restoration over time. *Make repair a non-negotiable part of your daily architecture.*

- **Give yourself permission to rest without guilt.** Rest is not laziness. It's not wasted time. It's not something you have to earn. Rest is a biological necessity, as essential as food and water. When you rest, you're not doing nothing, you're doing the most important maintenance work your body requires. *Release the guilt and embrace the wisdom.*

The truth is that small, consistent actions are much more effective than large, unsustainable efforts. You don't need to overhaul your entire routine. You need to build in simple practices that restore your body and mind day by day.

When you incorporate rest, your mornings begin refreshed. Your energy lasts without dramatic crashes. Work engages rather than depletes you. Your body feels lighter, more responsive. Your mind stays sharper throughout the day. You finish tasks with capacity remaining, not completely drained. Problems that seemed overwhelming become manageable. Relationships flow more smoothly. *Creative solutions emerge naturally.*

Thrive Principle: Rest & Repair

Rest is not the opposite of productivity. It is the foundation of it. When you restore what has deteriorated, you go beyond mere survival. You build the capacity to thrive for the long journey ahead.

PART 2:

THRIVING IN LIFE

You've done the essential work. You've laid the foundation, framed the walls, opened the windows, and weatherproofed against storms. The structure is sound. *It is resilient enough to hold you through anything.*

Now comes the question that changes everything: *What will you do with what you've built?*

Part One of this journey was about construction. You learned to build a resilient life that can withstand pressure, hold steady through uncertainty, and support your growth. You mastered the skills (or learned) the skills necessary to break ground, lay foundations, create frameworks, and maintain what you've created. Those skills matter deeply. They're what keep you standing when life shakes everything around you.

Part Two is about habitation. Living fully in the life you've built is crucial. Not just maintaining the structure, but filling it with joy, meaning, connection, and purpose. Moving from *doing* to genuinely *thriving*. This shift requires a different set of skills. Softer in nature, yet no less essential. You've learned how to be strong.

Now you'll learn to be present. To rest. To savour. *To allow enough to be enough.*

These upcoming chapters will guide you toward thriving. They will show you how to *live* and *love* what you have built.

The structure and framework are ready.

Time to learn to *love* living in it.

CHAPTER ELEVEN

Beyond Survival

The Shift to Thriving

The house is built. Foundation poured, the walls are framed, the windows are open, and the systems are in place. Here's the question no one asks: Are you loving *living* in it?

There's a profound difference between simply maintaining a structure and truly making it a home. It's the difference between checking the locks every night and lighting candles on the table. Between simply surviving in your space and thriving within it.

Dad taught me how to build strength. He demonstrated resilience through his work ethic, his determination, and his ability to push through almost anything. It took me years to learn that strength alone isn't the final goal. The true goal is living well in the life you've built.

For most of my father's life, he was in constant motion. He spent most of his life building businesses, making deals, solving problems, providing for his family, and fixing what was broken. Regardless of his emotions, he mastered the art of endurance, perseverance, and fulfilling his responsibilities. Thriving came later and it arrived quietly.

After his heart attack forced him to slow down, he experienced a significant shift in his life. Dad started sitting on the back porch in the evenings. He merely immersed himself in reading the evening paper. Not fixing, building, or planning. He was simply sitting and observing his surroundings evening light change. Listening to the neighbourhood sounds. Being still.

For a man who had built his entire identity on constant motion, this was revolutionary, for he rarely sat still. At first, I think he felt guilty about it, as if he should be accomplishing, producing, or proving something. Slowly, over months and years, he learned to just be. In those quiet evenings, I saw him thriving in a way that surpassed all his business success.

He wasn't just surviving anymore. He was savouring.

What Thriving Means

Surviving is about *endurance*. It means getting through the day, checking the boxes, managing the crises, maintaining composure, and holding everything together is the essence of survival. Proving to yourself and everyone else that you can handle whatever comes. Surviving asks, "*Can I make it through this?*"

Thriving asks something entirely different: *Am I actually living?*

There's nothing wrong with survival mode. Sometimes, it's exactly what we need. When you're in a crisis, when everything is falling apart, when you're barely keeping your head above water, survival skills are absolutely essential.

Dad's generation mastered these skills. As Depression-era kids, wartime survivors, and people who knew real hardship, they learned to endure, persist, and to never give up. They passed on an inheritance of incredible resilience, work ethic and grit... It is the capacity to overcome almost any obstacle.

What often wasn't passed down, however, was permission to enjoy. They couldn't teach us how to rest without guilt. To say *"this is enough"* without feeling lazy or to pursue joy without justifying it first. They knew how to survive, but not how to truly thrive.

Our parents deeply wanted us to thrive. Often, they simply didn't know how. They were too busy surviving to learn it themselves. Dad worked relentlessly his whole life. He provided everything we needed and most of what we wanted. He never complained, never *quit,* and never took the easy way out. He also never learned to receive. *To truly rest* or to just be without producing something.

The Shift From Building to Living

There's a precise moment in construction when the work changes character. The structure is sound. The systems are installed. The house can withstand the weather, hold its weight, and protect everything inside. At this point, a new kind of work begins.

You're no longer building for survival or stability; you're creating space for life to unfold.

You're choosing paint colours, arranging furniture, and deciding how lighting will move throughout the rooms. You're making decisions about how you want to feel when you come home, what matters enough to display, which spaces invite gathering, and which offer solitude.

Transitioning from construction to habitation requires an *entirely different mindset.*

The builder asks, *"Will this hold? Will this last? Will this protect?*

The dweller asks, *"Does this nourish me? Does this reflect who I am? Does this make room for joy?*

Neither question is more important than the other. You need both. The structure *must* be sound before you can truly live in it.

I spent so many years focused on building my life that I forgot to ask the second question: *Am I enjoying my life?* My focus seemed to be on proving I could handle anything, provide for my kids, and rebuild after everything fell apart. I was always so preoccupied making sure the structure wouldn't collapse that I forgot to actually *live* in what I was creating.

Thriving isn't constant happiness. It doesn't mean never struggling, having everything figured out, or reaching some perfect, finished state. Thriving is choosing *presence over productivity.* It involves finding meaning in ordinary moments. Celebrating progress, not just completion.

The Art of Cherishing What You've Built

Living aligned with what matters most, not what impresses others most, is the heart of thriving. *Thriving is joy woven into the structure, not added as a reward after all the work is done.*

You've used your incredible resilience to build something meaningful. The question now becomes: *How will you cherish it?*

Stories of Thriving

Dad's Porch Revolution

Every evening after dinner, Dad would head to the back porch to read the evening paper. Same chair. Same spot. The act of simply being present was his sacred ritual. Mom would sometimes join him, and they'd sit together in comfortable silence. Other times, he'd sit alone. Either way, he wasn't doing anything that looked productive. *He was just there, skimming the local news and gently petting the family dog.*

I remember one evening asking him what he did out there every night. He looked at me with genuine contentment and said,

"Nothing. It's perfect." For a man whose worth had been measured by output for nine decades, choosing to do nothing except read the local newspaper and pet the dog felt like the most radical act of self-indulgence I'd ever witnessed for him. He wasn't producing, achieving, or improving anything; he was simply being alive and *letting that be enough.*

That's when I began to understand the difference between surviving and thriving. Surviving meant constantly proving his value through work. Thriving meant *knowing* his value existed, whether he produced anything or not. Those porch evenings weren't wasted time. They reclaimed life. These were moments when Dad finally gave himself permission to exist without having to earn it.

My Saturday Morning Awakening

For years after leaving my marriage, I lived in pure survival mode. *Get this done. Do that. Pay the bills. Prove I could do this alone. Keep it all together.* Show everyone, including myself, that I was okay. I was resilient as hell. Yet, I was far from thriving.

The shift for me came on an ordinary Saturday morning. My daughter was home from university, attempting to make pancakes badly, with flour everywhere and batter dripping onto the floor. My son was home too, singing off-key in the bedroom, while getting dressed. The sun streamed through the kitchen window, illuminating the mess.

In that chaotic, imperfect moment, I realized I wasn't just getting through life. I was actually happy *in* my life. Not the dramatic happiness of major achievements, but the quiet, ordinary happiness of being present with my life. I was content to notice the flour-covered faces and laughter, rather than stressing out about the mess. I treasured hearing off-key singing and feeling grateful, not rushed. I felt a deep sense of fulfillment from within.

That's when I understood the difference. Surviving kept us fed, safe, and functional. Thriving meant noticing the beauty in the chaos and *choosing* to fully embrace it. The life I'd built, my new life, my new stability, and my resilient foundation were finally strong enough that I could simply live in it, inhabit it fully as myself and enjoy it unconditionally.

The Permission We Didn't Receive

For most of us, our parents taught us essential survival skills. Work hard. Be responsible. Provide for your family. Push through difficulty. Don't complain. *Don't quit.* These lessons saved us, shaped us, and gave us incredible grit. They made us who we are.

Yet, many didn't teach us how to rest without guilt, how to enjoy something without earning it first, or how to say *"This is enough"* and mean it. They didn't model how to choose joy when there was still work left to do.

Not because they were withholding something. Often, they just genuinely didn't know how. They were too busy surviving themselves to learn to thrive. Think about your parents' or grandparents' generation. Many grew up amidst hardship, economic depression, war, and scarcity. They learned early that life was hard, and they had to be harder. *Rest was a luxury.* Joy was something that happened after all the work was done, which meant it *rarely happened at all.*

Those foundational lessons served our parents well. They kept them alive and fed their families. *Built futures for us.* Yet, when survival mode becomes your only mode, it carries a profound cost. You never learn when enough is enough. Your worth is measured solely by your output, and you feel deep guilt about any pleasure not earned through suffering first. Even after you've already won, you simply don't know how to stop.

We inherited their strength, resilience, and incredible capacity to endure. We also inherited their guilt associated with taking breaks and rest. They believed that overcoming challenges is the only sign of worthiness. Their fear was that if they stop pushing, *everything* will fall apart.

Here's the gift we can give ourselves and the next generation: *We can honour everything our parents taught us about resilience by also choosing what they couldn't model. We can be both strong and rested. Productive and present. We can be both driven and content.* That's not rejecting their legacy. That's completing it. They survived so we could thrive. The best way to honour that legacy is by living every day, thriving in our lives.

Most of us were never taught how to thrive. We mastered survival skills beautifully, *but thriving?* That often feels unclear, unfamiliar, or even selfish. It's crucial to share the many ways thriving can show up in your life and the patterns and habits you can adopt that make thriving your new normal. Thriving is a constant practice. It's a beloved place to inhabit, not a destination to reach. My goal is simple, that the examples of thriving I share encourage you to see the benefits and begin thriving in every area of your life.

To truly thrive is to *fully commit to living.*

Thrive Patterns: Eight Shifts from Surviving to Thriving

Thriving requires intentionally shifting our focus from relentless survival to mindful living. These are the powerful habits that make thriving your new normal.

Notice the good as quickly as you spot the problems.

Your brain is naturally wired to scan for threats. That's the survival instinct that kept your ancestors alive. Thriving demands intentionally retraining your attention toward what's working, what's beautiful, and what's already here and worth celebrating. Problems will always announce themselves. *Joy requires you to look for it.*

Let 'Enough' Be Enough.

Survival mode whispers constantly: *More, better, faster, prove yourself, keep going.* Thriving whispers back: *You're already whole.* What you have, who you are, and what you've built is enough right now. You can rest there. You can let that be your ground. *Growth can happen through sufficiency, not just scarcity.*

Choose Presence Over Productivity.

Survival asks at day's end: *What did you accomplish? What did you check off the list?*

Thriving asks, "*Were you actually there for any of it? Did you feel the sun on your face, taste your food, hear the laughter, or notice the small moments that make up a life?*

Presence is the price of admission to a thriving life. *Without it, you're just moving through your days, not living them.*

Celebrate Progress, Not Just Completion.

Survival mode only counts wins when you cross the finish line, and the destination is all that matters. Thriving celebrates every step along the way, every attempt, showing up, learning, and the courage to try again after failing. The small improvements are often overlooked by others. Progress is thriving in motion.

Say *Yes* To Joy Without Earning It First.

You don't have to finish everything on your to-do list before you rest. You don't have to be perfect before you play. You don't have to suffer to earn the right to pleasure. Joy isn't a reward for good behaviour. It's fuel for the journey. That's what makes the work sustainable. Stop treating pleasure like a dessert that only comes after the work is done or only after you finish your vegetables. *Let it nourish you along the way.*

Build Rhythms Of Rest Into Your Structure.

Surviving treats rest as collapse, something you do when you literally cannot go on any longer. Thriving treats rest as strategic, something you do regularly so you can keep going well. Dad's daily nap after his heart attack wasn't a weakness. It was wisdom. Choose sustainable energy over constant depletion. Rest isn't productivity. *It's the foundation of it.*

Let Relationships Be The Point, Not The Task.

Survival mode checks the relationship box: *Called Mom. Helped kids with homework. Had a date night. Box checked.* Thriving mode asks deeper questions: *Did I actually connect? Was I truly engaged, or was I merely going through the motions? Did love move between us, or did we just manage logistics?* Relationships aren't tasks to complete, they are *the reason we built the house in the first place.*

Ask Honest Questions.

Survival deflects, "It's all their fault. This is always happening to me. No one wants me to succeed. What did I ever do to deserve this? Thriving is brave, it asks, "Why is this happening to me? What can I do to make it better? What can I learn from this for my future? What was my role, and am I capable of doing better next time?" Honest questions that yield candid answers will help you thrive long-term.

The Invitation Forward

Don't just maintain the structure you've built. *Live in it.* Fill those rooms with laughter, with presence, and with deep meaning. Move freely through the spaces you've created and make them be the very essence of you.

Thriving is something you choose. Daily. In small ways. *In the ordinary moments* of the life you're already living right now. Your parents taught you to survive, and that gift cannot be overstated. Their resilience *lives* in you. Now, you're learning to do something they often couldn't: You're learning to thrive. Strive to build a life that is both strong and joyful. Your life should be functional as well as meaningful. Not just enduring, but flourishing.

Both matter. Both honour the work and respect the struggle. Survival skills keep you standing. Thriving skills make standing worthwhile. You've built the house with a strong foundation and solid walls. *Now live in it. Really live in it.*

That's what the next chapters are about. Not just how to keep the structure standing, but how to fill it with the warmth, connection, purpose, and daily practices that transform a shelter into a home. You've earned this. You've built for this. Now give yourself permission.

Thrive Principle: Beyond Survival

Resilience builds the foundation. Thriving is the choice to live joyfully in what you've created. You've earned the right. Now give yourself permission.

CHAPTER TWELVE

The Art of Contentment

Contentment as Steady Ground

I was speaking with a friend the other day, and she mentioned something that really struck me and got me thinking. *"Contentment is the new currency of success,"* she said.

We were discussing how much has shifted in what people value, what they're chasing, and what truly matters when you strip away all the noise. Material possessions and accolades used to hold a prominent place in people's priorities for a long time and sit at the top of their list. *The corner office. An impressive title. The house that makes the neighbours jealous.* Now, people are seeking something deeper. A fundamental sense of peace and contentment. Finding satisfaction in their lives that doesn't depend on what they own or achieve.

I thought about that conversation for days afterward. I thought about Dad, who understood this essential truth long before it became trendy. I thought about my own journey from chasing what looked impressive to discovering what actually *fills you up*. We can build the strongest foundations and learn to thrive, yet without genuine contentment underneath, it all, the entire structure feels hollow. You've made it this far. You've enhanced your resilience, opened yourself up, and started shifting from survival to thriving. Now comes the critical question that determines whether all that work leads to peace or just more striving: *Can you let what you've built be enough? Can you rest in it? Can you find contentment right here, in the imperfect present you're actually living, instead of waiting for some imagined perfect future?*

Contentment is different from other qualities. You can't force contentment, schedule it, or make it stay. It comes and goes and requires nurturing to settle in and grow. Contentment resides at the core of your *being.* The steady hum. Even the quiet knowing when happiness leaves the room, you're still okay. You still have enough. *You still are enough.*

Dad used to say, *"Nine out of ten things you worry about never happen."* He wasn't dismissing real problems. He was pointing to something deeper: most of our suffering comes from the stories we tell ourselves, not the reality we're living. Contentment is the art of learning to rest in what's real, instead of clinging to what hasn't happened yet. It's the essential practice of knowing and trusting in what *is,* not what is imagined.

Before I learned this art, I spent most of my twenties anxious, catastrophizing everything. If I made one mistake at work, I'd spiral: *I'll get fired, I won't be able to pay rent, and I'll end up homeless.* The whole disaster played out in vivid detail in my mind, complete with worst-case scenarios I'd never actually face.

Dad would listen patiently, then ask, *"Has that happened yet?"*

"No, but it could," I'd reply.

"Nine out of ten things you worry about never happen," he would say in a patient tone.

I hated that phrase at first. It felt dismissive, as though he didn't understand real anxiety and the weight of what-ifs that kept me awake at night. Decades later, I started tracking my worries. Writing them down in a journal, then checking back three months later to see which ones had actually materialized. Dad was right. Maybe ninety-five percent never came true. The suffering was real, but the threat wasn't.

The worry consumed hours of my life, drained my energy, and shaped my decisions. These concerns were all based on scenarios that only existed in my imagination. Now, when I catch myself spiralling, I pause. I ask, *"Is this happening right now, or am I imagining it?"* Most of the time, it's imagination or overreaction. In that pause, contentment has room to return. Because the future's safety is never guaranteed, I calm myself by focusing on the precious moments of contentment in my current life.

Whether it's a month, a week, or a day, I find what is true, real, and tangible, and I focus my attention and contentment on that reality.

The Soil and the Flower

If happiness is the flower blooming, then contentment is the soil it grows from. Both matter. Both are beautiful. They support one another, and both rely on each other for strength. One is stunning, the other is long-lasting. Only contentment sustains you through all seasons, allowing you to *love the life you have built for yourself* and enabling you to thrive over and over again.

When contentment becomes your ground, everything else shifts. Setbacks don't destroy you because your worth depends on more than outcomes. Disappointments hurt but don't define you, because your sense of peace doesn't depend on everything going right. Success feels sweeter because you're not desperately chasing it to prove something. You can celebrate without clinging, work hard without burning out, and want more without feeling incomplete.

Throughout my years of pursuing contentment and peace and cultivating the necessary inner soil, I have observed a profound paradox between our desires and what we truly achieve. The *Contentment Paradox* works like this: the more you chase happiness, the more elusive it becomes. Conversely, when you cultivate contentment, when you simply rest in what is, happiness visits more often. Not because you've demanded it, but because you've created space for it.

Dad modelled this philosophy earnestly. He didn't have the biggest house, the fanciest car, or the most impressive title. He had mornings with his newspaper and coffee. He had family dinners. He had work he believed in. He was deeply content. His contentment wasn't a result of having everything, but because he genuinely appreciated what he had built and discovered the constant treasures it brought.

Imagine how much better the world would be if we could simply *rest in the contentment* of what we've already built.

The Enough Moment

After my divorce I moved into a small rental house with two bedrooms. We'd lost the big house, the yard, and the life I'd built. I felt like I'd failed everyone. I felt like I had failed at providing my kids with the stability they deserved, the home they knew, and the intact family I couldn't keep together.

One evening my sister and I were eating pizza on the floor surrounded by a few unpacked boxes, because I didn't have a dining table yet. Everything was out of place, and we had almost nothing. My sister looked up, cheese on her chin, and said, "*This is really fun, MJ. It feels like we're glamping.*"

That's when it hit me. Contentment wasn't the big house; *it was simply being together with family.* Contentment wasn't waiting for some future when I 'got back on my feet' or 'rebuilt what we'd lost.' I could instantly enjoy eating floor pizza with my sister right there.

That was the moment it hit me. I stopped measuring my life against what I'd left behind and *started living forward with what I was now building.*

I quickly realized I'd been so focused on what we didn't have that I'd missed what we did have: *each other, safety, a fresh start, and the possibility of building something new.* That shift in perspective didn't erase the loss or make the divorce less painful. It simply reminded me that contentment lives in how we see what's in front of us, not in waiting for circumstances to change.

It was up to me to find new ways, simpler ways, perhaps, to cultivate a greater understanding of contentment in my life.

Dad's Mornings of Contentment

Looking back at my childhood, I could see that our home modelled contentment. Most mornings, Dad would sit at the kitchen table with his coffee and newspaper. Mom would hum in the background as she prepared breakfast and made coffee. *Nothing fancy.* Nothing Instagram™-worthy. There was nothing that anyone would write about or photograph. Just ordinary time, unhurried and *present.*

I'd wander in, still half-asleep, and he'd look up with this expression of complete satisfaction. *"This is the good life,"* he'd say. Every single morning. The same words, the same contentment.

Dad felt this not during big deals, milestones, or recognition, but in these ordinary and unremarkable moments. That *was* contentment. He wasn't waiting for big wins to feel successful, he found richness and deep reward in the simple, reliable routine of an ordinary morning. That helped me understand that a good life isn't always dramatic or exciting. Sometimes it's just coffee, a newspaper, and the people you love nearby.

Those mornings shaped how I define thriving now. It's not about the peaks, the achievements, or the moments worth posting about. It's about the ordinary days you actually live in. The quiet contentment that doesn't need anything more to feel complete.

Thrive Patterns: Eight Practices for Cultivating Contentment

It's one thing to say you are content and another to intentionally practice it actively in your life. Contentment doesn't just show up, it must be cultivated. To help foster more peace and contentment in you and your life, here are eight actionable practices I subscribe to that can make a difference on your own contentment scale. As I've said before, it doesn't just show up; it needs to be cultivated.

Choose one of these suggestions and commit to using one consistently and intentionally to find the deep contentment you deserve.

Savour the Ordinary.

Notice the warmth of your coffee in the morning. Observe the light streaming through your window or the small kindnesses that fill your day. *Contentment grows with attention to what's already here.* Most of life happens in ordinary moments. If you wait for extraordinary experiences to feel content, you will miss out on most of your life. *Train your attention toward the unremarkable beauty that constantly surrounds you.*

Practice the Pause Before the Spiral.

When worry starts, stop. Ask yourself: *"Is this real or imagined? Is this happening right now, or am I rehearsing for a future that may never come?"* Most suffering lives in projection, not presence. The pause creates space between the trigger and the spiral. In that space, you can choose contentment over catastrophe. *You can return to what's actually true right now instead of rehearsing a future that may never come.*

Let Enough Be Enough.

You don't need *more* to be good enough, and you don't need *a lot* to be worthy. What you have, who you are, and where you are right now can be your tilled soil. Start there. *Let that be sufficient. This doesn't mean you stop growing or wanting or working, but grow from a place of wholeness rather than lack, and from gratitude rather than grasping.*

Celebrate the Wins You Already Have.

Healthy kids. A roof overhead. Work that matters. Friendships that sustain you. These aren't 'just' the basics. They're everything. Name them. Thank them. Write them down. Speak them out loud. The practice of naming what's working trains your brain to notice abundance instead of constantly scanning for what's missing. *Celebrate these gifts in big and small ways to lock in the emotion of appreciating the ones you already possess.*

Befriend the Present Moment.

Stop living in *"when I finally..."* or *"back when I used to..."* The only life you actually have is *this one, right now.* Thriving happens right here, or it happens nowhere. The past is gone and the future is imagined. This moment, whatever it holds, is all that's real. *Contentment lives in learning to be here fully, not half-present while wishing you were somewhere else.*

Release the Scoreboard.

Stop yourself from measuring your life against others. Their success isn't relevant to yours. Contentment dies in comparison. Your reality is richer than you think when you stop comparing. Contentment lives in being fully aware and thrives in the appreciation of your unique path, your specific blessings, and your particular journey. *No one else is living your life. Stop judging yours by someone else's standards and create your own.*

Choose Gratitude as a Reflex.

Train your brain to notice the good instead of reflexively spotting problems. *What went right today? Who showed up? What small beauty crossed your path?* This positivity will override the attention toward whatever you are struggling with. The intentional focus on positivity will override the attention toward whatever you are struggling with, preventing the struggle from becoming the main narrative. Gratitude is a muscle. *The more you use it, the stronger it becomes.*

Trust the Unfolding.

Life moves at its own pace. Fighting the timing exhausts you. Contentment grows when you stop forcing the process and start dancing with it. Sometimes, things take longer than you want. Some arrive sooner than expected. Some never come at all. *Trusting the unfolding doesn't mean you stop working toward what you want. It means you stop suffering over the timeline.*

The Gift of Contentment

Contentment is always available to you at any time throughout your life. Not because life is perfect, but because you've learned to trust in what is, find sufficiency in the present, and let enough be enough. Happiness will come and go; that's its nature. Chase it, and you'll exhaust yourself running after something that moves faster than you do. Wait for it, and you'll miss the life you're living while you wait.

Dad's generation survived by pushing through, working harder, and never stopping. We inherited that incredible strength, that capacity to endure almost anything. While they didn't always teach us how to rest in what we've built or be content with it, they certainly taught us that if you want anything in life, you need to work for it. Contentment is the same. It requires your attention, focus, and commitment. Our parents used that powerful driving work ethic to bring about a greater experience of *inner peace and contentment.*

The best news is you can have both: the resilience to build a wonderful life and the contentment to enjoy what you've created. That's *thriving*. That's understanding the difference between the foundation that holds you and the momentary joys that light up your days. You get both. The steady ground and the bright moments. Contentment and happiness are like soil and flowers. It's all for you to enjoy.

Contentment is not settling for less. It does not involve giving up on growth, denying problems, or pasting on fake positivity. *Contentment is a deep acceptance of what is,* while still working toward what could be. It's gratitude for the present without clinging to it. It's peace that doesn't depend on external circumstances. It's the ability to say, "*This is enough, thank you.*"

Thrive Principle: The Art of Contentment

Contentment isn't the absence of desire. It's the presence of peace with what is, even as you work toward what could be. It's the foundation that lets everything else bloom.

CHAPTER THIRTEEN

Thriving Through Connection

Mastering Relationships

You can build the strongest house in the world, complete with a perfect foundation, solid walls, and storm-proof windows. But if no one ever comes inside, if no warmth ever fills those rooms, and laughter never echoes off those walls, *what's the point?*

Houses are built for people. *Lives are built for connection.* Thriving doesn't happen in isolation. It happens in relationships in the friction and forgiveness of daily life together. It happens in the messy and beautiful process of letting people in, even when it's hard and even when it hurts.

Dad knew this well. His relationships weren't perfect. Sometimes even he and I clashed, misunderstood each other, and disappointed each other. Yet, he never stopped showing up. He never stopped choosing connection over being right.

That's what I call an emotionally storm-proofed life. It's not about the absence of conflict, but the commitment to work through it.

Storm-Proofing Through Friction and Forgiveness

Every close relationship has friction. Different needs, perspectives, communication styles, and expectations about how things should be. The question isn't whether friction will come, but what you do with it when it arrives. You have two paths. You can let friction harden into resentment, slowly eroding the relationship, or you can transform friction into understanding, allowing the connection and relationship to *strengthen through the working-through.*

Emotional storm-proofing means building internal stability so external conflict doesn't destroy the connection. It means you can disagree without disconnecting. You can agree to disagree. You can feel hurt without becoming hardened. You can be disappointed without destroying what you have built together. You can need space without severing ties completely.

The real work of *emotional storm-proofing* happens in moments most people never see. You must catch yourself before you say something you can't take back. Choosing *repair over being right* when your ego desperately wants the win. Giving people the space to be human, imperfect, and evolving is more important than demanding they meet standards you can't even meet yourself. *Forgiving quickly,* before resentment roots so deep it becomes part of the foundation. Returning to connection after conflict instead of letting the distance become permanent.

Mastering emotional storm-proofing matters for *thriving* because without it, isolation can set in, or even worse, self-judgment and self-blame. The truth is, connection and vulnerability often mean putting our emotions at risk. It means being exposed, being vulnerable, and being disappointed at times. But it also means being real, genuine, and human, and real connections are absolutely essential for a full life.

Your capacity to navigate friction in connections ultimately determines your relationship depth. People who can only handle surface-level pleasantness will only have surface-level relationships. *Storm-proofed relationships* become your greatest source of joy and meaning precisely because they've been tested and held. They endure where others wither, and they often strengthen and even improve as a result of the storm.

Growing up, my father-daughter relationship had its handful of storms. Dad wasn't perfect, and I certainly wasn't perfect either. Occasionally, we hurt each other, misunderstood each other, and repeatedly disappointed each other's expectations. Yet, through it all, we kept *choosing connections.* We persevered through the challenges without allowing them to undermine the foundation we had established. We worked through the storm and didn't let it destroy what we had built. That commitment made the relationship invaluable to me, and it forms the basis of this book and my bond with you.

My Own Storm-Proofing Practice

When I was weathering the massive storm in my own life, I had every reason to close myself off to my father and my entire family. I wanted to build walls high enough so that no one could ever hurt me again. For a time, I decided people weren't safe, relationships weren't worth the risk, and *independence was the only protection that mattered.*

But I had watched Dad emotionally *storm-proof* his relationships my whole life. I saw him choose connection, even when it was hard, painful, or easier to walk away. His example helped me make a different choice: *not isolation.* I persevered through my fear and decided I needed to let people in. I did so slowly and carefully, establishing better boundaries than I'd had before. I *chose to make new connections* and did so genuinely and intentionally.

Some friendships weathered the storms of my life falling apart. Some didn't. Some people simply couldn't handle the mess, the uncertainty, or the reality that I was no longer the person they'd known. The ones that held on, the ones that chose to stay and work through the awkwardness, grief, and rebuilding with me; those became the *essential beams holding my life up* when everything else felt shaky.

Thriving wasn't about surviving alone or proving I could make it without anyone. *Thriving was risking connection even after I'd been hurt.* It was learning to trust again without being naive and building relationships that could hold friction without falling apart. I am still learning, choosing, and committing to this practice, even when it feels uncomfortable, because I know the reward on the other side is magnificent.

Dad showed me that.

The Dementia Years

Some of my greatest challenges with Dad came when his mind started slipping due to dementia. It was then our roles were reversed in ways I never imagined. The man who had always been our family's rock, the one everyone turned to for answers, suddenly needed help remembering names, finding words, and navigating the profound confusion that would descend without warning.

Some days Dad would look at me with frustration, *"Why are you telling me what to do?"* This made me feel like I was overstepping instead of helping, or like I was the problem instead of the solution. I could have easily taken it personally. I could have let the hurt harden into distance or pulled back to protect myself from the sting of his confusion.

Instead, I remembered everything I'd learned about *emotional storm-proofing.* This was still Dad. He was just *scared.* He was just trying to make sense of a mind that no longer worked the way it once did. I saw the human being in him, facing something terrifying with whatever dignity he could still muster.

Emotional storm-proofing in those years meant showing up even when he didn't remember why I was there. I made a conscious decision to prioritize our connection over my personal discomfort in witnessing his decline. Loving him not for who he used to be, but for who he still was in that moment. Forgiving any sharp words that came from fear, not malice, and holding the relationship steady when his grip on reality loosened.

Those years taught me something profound about thriving through connection. Real love isn't just being there when it's easy. It's showing up when every instinct tells you to protect yourself.

It's staying when the person you're connecting with can't fully connect back. That's when *storm-proofing* matters most. That's when you discover that what you built is something you truly cherish and it is absolutely worth fighting for.

The Dishes and the Lawn

Through all the good times and challenging times with Dad, the most important thing was the security of our connection. Emotions would come and go, but the foundation we had was cemented through the wisdom, generational connection, and resilience he instilled in me. I'll admit that our foundation was sometimes seriously rocked. Like all children, I tested Dad, and he tested me. I learned early on at a young age that our relationship wasn't supposed to be perfect. It would be tested, and what mattered was that we endured.

One particular disagreement lives in my memory like a freeze-frame. I can still see it even now, decades later. My brothers were sitting around the kitchen table staring at me, and my father held a fork in his hand. As dinner came to an end, a debate erupted over gender roles and female equality. Dad's face became red with frustration, plus he had just had a very stressful day at the office, between business dealings. My timing wasn't the greatest, but my teenage fury and self-righteousness were burning.

The night before, I had an engaging conversation with my extended family about women's liberation around the dining room table and I was eager to apply these new concepts at home. The very next evening, when it came time to clear the table, I decided to test the waters on my own family. I intervened and proposed that perhaps my sister, Mom, and I should remain seated, while my brothers could take responsibility for cleaning up and doing the dishes, for a change.

Dad's words hung in the air between us: *"You want equality? Fine. Clear the dishes, AND while you're at it, you can mow the lawn, too."*

I was furious and I felt utterly betrayed. That was it; I was running away from home! Here was my progressive father, my hero, the man who'd spent dinner the night before discussing women's liberation and equal rights for everyone. Now he was revealing what he *really* thought: I should stay in my feminine lane. He believed that I was 'just one of the girls.' His liberal talk about women's rights was apparently negotiable when it came to his own household. Those intellectual beliefs were fine for debate, but in his home, traditional roles still ruled. As I fought back with my opinion, he punished me with double the chores and what he deemed as 'man's work.' I could now do both!

I was so angry I could barely look at him. The fury wasn't just about chores. It was about hypocrisy. About realizing the person I'd trusted most could hold contradictory beliefs. I knew Dad was stressed and his business pressures were mounting, but I felt foolish for blindly and completely believing in his words when his actions told an entirely different story and contradicted them.

The following weeks and months, things were slightly different between us. Mom encouraged us to keep the lines of communication open between us because the economic times were becoming increasingly challenging and affecting Dad's business. She said Dad didn't need any additional pressures at home right now.

Then, our foundation kicked in, our deep connection and *emotional storm-proofing* helped shift things. Dad and I stopped allowing any tension to fester. We talked. I listened to him, though not always in a well-informed or patient manner. Yet, slowly, I saw something I'd missed in my fury. Dad *was* trying. Caught between what he believed intellectually and what felt cohesive from his generation's conditioning. He was fighting against patterns so deeply ingrained that he didn't even see them as patterns.

Soon enough, I started giving him the grace I wanted for myself. I found room to evolve in the imperfect situation. I found the space to acknowledge his contradictions without diminishing them. We gave each other permission to be human while still being held accountable.

Years later, Dad apologized for that night. It was not a dramatic scene. He simply took the opportunity to engage in a quiet, private conversation during which he stated, "*I was wrong to dismiss you like that. You were right to challenge me.*"

That became the moment I knew that when we developed a powerful emotional connection, nothing outside of us could weaken it. By *storm-proofing* our connections for those inevitable moments, we ensure relationship longevity. If we can't avoid the storm, we rebuild after it passes. We don't pretend conflict didn't happen, but we instead refuse to let it define the relationship. We don't demand perfection, but we do require understanding. The relationship will hold when we choose to stay in it, to work through the friction, and to *honour* it.

Thrive Patterns: Eight Ways to Storm-Proof Your Relationships

Relationships are one of the trickiest and yet most rewarding connections we can ever make in life. Cultivating a positive, healthy relationship requires that we work on ourselves first. When we shift, everyone shifts around us, and when we improve and act differently, everyone else has to respond differently.

I've found that the hardest relationships require learning and adapting, not from them, but from me. Since I can control my actions, not theirs, I have the ability to build a framework that makes sure my connections elevate me. That requires *emotional storm-proofing* your relationships and steps to improve my own reactions and behaviours.

Here are eight strategies you can use to enjoy *emotionally storm-proofing* your relationships so that they cultivate connections that thrive and last.

Name The Friction Before It Explodes.

Small irritations become big resentments when ignored. Say it early, say it kindly: "*This is bothering me. Can we talk?*" The goal isn't to eliminate friction. It's to address it while it's still small, while you can still approach it with curiosity instead of defensiveness. *Most relationship damage happens from accumulated small hurts, not single big betrayals.*

Choose Repair Over Being Right.

You can win the argument and lose the relationship. You can prove your point and damage trust. You can be correct and be alone. *Which matters more? Being right, or being connected?* This doesn't mean you never stand up for yourself or let everything slide. *It means to choose your relationship over your ego most of the time.*

Give People Room to Be Imperfect.

Including yourself. Mistakes aren't betrayals. They're human. Respond with curiosity, not condemnation. Ask "*What were you thinking?*" instead of "*How could you?*" Assume good intent until proven otherwise. People mess up. They disappoint expectations. They have awful days where they're not their best selves. *Grace in those moments builds relationships that can hold you through your own worst days.*

Practice Forgiveness As Prevention.

Don't let small hurts accumulate into mountains of resentment. Release them quickly, before they harden into grudges you'll carry for years. Forgiveness isn't for them. *It's for you.* It's refusing to let someone else's mistake take up permanent residence in your heart. Quick forgiveness doesn't mean you forget or pretend it didn't happen. Forgiveness is freeing. *It means you process the hurt and let it go instead of building your identity around being wounded.*

Build During Calm Periods, Not Just Crises.

Storm-proof during sunny weather. Create rituals of connection when things are good, so the structure holds when things get hard. Regular check-ins. Shared meals. Meaningful conversations that go beneath the surface. Time spent together isn't about managing logistics. *These deposits into the relationship account matter most when you need to make withdrawals during difficult seasons.*

Stay When It's Uncomfortable.

The urge to flee during conflict is strong. Every instinct screams to protect yourself by leaving. Growth happens in the staying. Choosing to be present instead of avoiding situations is the key to growth. Growth happens when you choose to sit with discomfort.

Try sitting long enough to work through it, instead of running the moment things get hard. While some relationships aren't worth the cost of staying. *Most connections are worth the discomfort and friction required to work through them.*

Let People Evolve.

Who they were five years ago isn't who they are now. Who they are now isn't who they'll be five years from now. Allow growth. Celebrate change. Don't freeze people in past versions of themselves. Don't hold them to mistakes they've already grown beyond. Don't expect them to stay static while you're allowed to evolve. *Storm-proofing means building relationships flexible enough to hold change.*

Return to Connection After Conflict.

Rupture is inevitable. Repair is optional. Always choose repair. Always find your way back to each other. The relationship survives because you reconcile after fights. It survives because you always come back, because you refuse to let distance become permanent. This is due to your steadfast refusal to allow distance. Connection matters more than pride. *That choice, made repeatedly, is what storm-proofers love.*

Where Thriving Lives

Thriving requires letting people in. Risking the mess, navigating the frictions, and choosing connections even when it's hard, are essential for thriving. Dad taught me resilience through his work ethic and determination. He taught me how to thrive through his relationships. Relationships are imperfect and honest, and they are storm-proofed by commitment, forgiveness, and the daily decision to show up.

The strongest structure in the world is nothing without the warmth of people filling it. The most resilient life is lonely without connection. Be willing to storm-proof your relationships. This is not about avoiding conflict, but rather about developing the internal strength to navigate through it without destroying what truly matters. That's where thriving lives. In the space between friction and forgiveness. The decision to remain, to mend, and to reestablish connections, regardless of the number of storms encountered, is what defines thriving.

Relationships aren't what you *add* to a thriving life. They're where thriving happens. The daily act of showing up is where thriving occurs. In the vulnerability of being seen. In the risk of being hurt and the courage to stay anyway. In the grace of forgiving and being forgiven. In the commitment to choose each other, again and again, through every season.

That's the house worth building. Not one you live in alone, but one filled with people who matter. People you've weathered storms with. People who've seen you at your worst and stayed. People whose imperfections you hold gently because they hold yours the same way. That's not just a connection. *That's what thriving is all about.*

Thriving Through Connection

Thriving doesn't happen in isolation. It happens in the messy, beautiful work of connection, in relationships storm-proofed by commitment, grace, and the courage to choose each other again.

CHAPTER FOURTEEN

Generational Thriving

Breaking Old Patterns

I was having coffee with my daughter last month when she said something that stopped me mid-sip. *"Mom, you're allowed to rest. You know that, right?"* She was watching me check my phone for the third time in ten minutes, mentally running through everything I still needed to do that day. Her words hit me harder than they should have. Here I was, decades into my journey of learning to thrive, yet I still carried this gnawing guilt whenever I wasn't producing *enough or anything.*

That's when I realized: this isn't just *my* struggle. This *is* generational. The patterns our parents lived, the beliefs they passed down, and the survival skills that kept them going don't just disappear because we understand them intellectually. They live in our bodies. In our reflexes. In the voice that whispers, *"you're being lazy"* when you sit down to rest.

It is pretty safe to say your parents taught you to survive. They gave you strength, resilience, and the ability to endure the way that they were shown and taught. It's then safe to deduce that those lessons got you here, to where you are right now. Ultimately, those lessons shaped you and got you here and made you capable of building the life you have today. The question now becomes: *Did they also teach you to thrive? To rest without guilt? Did they also teach you to enjoy without having to earn it? To say "this is enough" without feeling like you're settling?*

More often than not, the answer is no. Not because they didn't want to or they didn't care. But, because they didn't *know how.* They were too busy surviving to learn to thrive themselves. And because their parents, your grandparents, didn't teach them how to thrive, either.

When Survival Becomes the Only Story

I have shared already how Dad's generation lived through the Great Depression, wars, and extreme economic hardship. Those situations profoundly shaped how he and those from that era saw the world. They mastered survival skills that kept families fed, roofs overhead, and ensured safety, but they didn't always cultivate emotional needs. Sure, they worked harder than everyone else. Maybe they never complained, and for some, many pushed through a great deal of pain. Most parents of that time provided for their families at all costs and investing in the joys of life was a luxury they couldn't afford.

The good news is, these skills kept them alive and built the foundation we now stand on. We owe them everything for their strength, relentless determination, and refusal to give up, regardless of what life threw at them. Yet, when survival mode becomes your only mode, it carries costs we don't always see until we're living it ourselves.

Growing up, I absorbed Dad's lessons about his generation without even realizing it. The way he handled setbacks. The way he never complained. The way work always came first, always mattered most, and always defined whether the day was successful. I learned that rest was something you did when everything else was finished, which meant *it almost never happened*. I learned that your value came from what you produced, not from who you were. I saw that joy was nice, but optional, while work was necessary and primary.

These weren't lessons Dad sat me down to teach. They were lessons I absorbed by watching his actions. By seeing what he praised and what he dismissed, noticing what made him proud and what made him uncomfortable, and understanding, without words, that certain ways of being were acceptable and others were signs of weakness.

The inheritance I gained from him and his generational conditioning wasn't just strength. It was also the limitations of that strength. The places where survival skills, however necessary they were for Dad's generation, didn't quite fit the life I was trying to build. I needed the resilience he taught me, but I also needed permission to rest, a permission he couldn't give because he'd never given it to himself.

He never learned to rest because rest felt dangerous, like everything would fall apart the moment he stopped moving. He measured worth by output because that's the only metric that kept him safe. He felt guilty for joy because pleasure wasn't something he believed he could get through anything other than endless work. He didn't know how to stop even when he'd already won, because stopping meant being exposed again. He taught his children to survive brilliantly, but he couldn't openly emulate thriving *because he never learned it himself.*

I watched this with Dad. His incredible work ethic, his ability to push through anything, and his determination to provide no matter the cost. I inherited all of it. That strength lives in me. I also inherited the guilt about rest and the discomfort with ease. I held the belief that overcoming challenges somehow elevated my worth and I feared that if I stopped pushing, everything I'd built would crumble.

The good news is, there came a time in my life when I didn't want that for myself anymore and certainly didn't want to continue the pattern and impose it on my kids. I made a firm decision that what I would teach my children about thriving would have to be something I had learned *myself.*

The Turning Point

My turning point came not in one dramatic moment but in a thousand small ones. It started with watching my kids grow up and realizing I was passing down the same patterns. Seeing my daughter push herself to exhaustion trying to do everything perfectly, just like I had. Noticing my son's confusion when I couldn't just sit and be with him because my mind was always on the next task.

One evening, my daughter asked if we could watch a movie together. I said *"yes,"* then spent the entire movie on my laptop, half-present at best. Afterward, she said quietly, *"You weren't really here, were you?"* That question broke something open in me. I was repeating the pattern, working constantly, proving my worth through output, and unable to just be present without feeling guilty about all the things I wasn't doing.

I thought about Dad's later years, after his heart attack forced him to slow down. How he finally learned to sit on the porch, read, and *just be.* How that shift came not from wisdom but from his body refusing to allow him to continue the way he'd always lived. I didn't want to wait for a crisis to give myself permission to thrive. I didn't want my kids to inherit the same guilt, the same relentless drive, and the same inability to rest that had defined so much of my life.

That's when I started making different choices. Small ones at first. Sitting through a movie without my laptop. Taking a walk without it being *"exercise with a purpose."* I learned to say no to things that didn't align with my priorities, even when it was uncomfortable to do so. I learned to rest before I collapsed, not as a reward for completing everything.

The guilt didn't disappear overnight. That voice that said, *"you're being lazy,"* still showed up. I started recognizing it for what it was: an inherited pattern, not an absolute truth. My worth didn't. It's not easy to be a bridge, a lighthouse, and a beacon of change in a system that seemed to work for so long. There's guilt in enjoying life when your parents never could. There's discomfort in self-care when they sacrificed so much. There's the constant question: *am*

I honouring their legacy or betraying it? The answer I've come to is this: honouring their legacy means using the strength they gave you to build something they couldn't quite reach. Completing the work they started, showing them, and yourself, that *their survival made your thriving possible.* They laid the foundation for the life you *get* to build. They gave you the tools to use to create something magnificent. That's to be honored and respected. They forged so that we could thrive and we will forge in our own ways so the next generation can thrive in ways we may never see.

My father's strength lives in me just as my strength lives on in my children. And my permission to thrive, live free, and enjoy life beautifully lives in me so it can live in them and their children. That is the power we have to set the tone for the generational wisdom we leave behind. Both are vital. Both are necessary for my productivity. I didn't have to earn the right to rest. I could be both strong *and* still. I could be both capable and content. Both my father's daughter and my own person.

How I'm Inspiring Differently

Now when my daughter pushes herself too hard, I tell her something no one told me at her age. *"You don't have to be perfect. You don't have to do everything. You're allowed to rest. Your worth isn't measured by your output."* She looks at me sometimes like I've given her permission to breathe, which I suppose I have.

When my son feels guilty about taking time for himself, I remind him that joy isn't something you earn after you've suffered enough.

It's part of a balanced life. It's fuel, not reward. These conversations feel like breaking a generational pattern in real-time. I'm teaching them what I'm still learning myself: how to honor the resilience our family is known for while also claiming the softness that makes life worth living.

This isn't rejecting Dad's lessons. *This is building on them.* Taking his incredible strength and adding the layer he couldn't quite reach. He survived so I could thrive. The best way to honour that is by actually thriving, by showing my kids there's another way, and by proving that you can hold both survival skills and thriving skills at once.

Some days I do this well. Some days I fall back into old patterns, checking my phone compulsively, feeling guilty about resting, and measuring my day by what I accomplished rather than how I felt. Progress isn't linear. I'm now aware of the pattern and can see when I'm living in survival mode versus thriving mode. I can make different choices, even when those choices feel uncomfortable.

The Bridge Generation

Perhaps that's what our generation is meant to be: the bridge. We inherited essential *survival* skills from parents who needed them desperately. We're learning the *thriving* skills our children will need more than ever in this constantly changing world. We are the ones translating between two landscapes of work and enjoyment, honoring what came before while consciously creating what comes next.

Both honour the full complexity of what it means to live well and thrive eternally. For ourselves and all the generations to come after us.

Thrive Patterns: Eight Ways to Break Survival Patterns and Choose Thriving

Breaking generational patterns isn't about rejecting what your parents taught you. It's about recognizing which patterns still serve you and which ones you've outgrown. It's about taking the best of what you inherited and adding what was missing. It is about consciously choosing to live differently than you were taught to shift the trajectory of what the next generation can learn from you.

Here are the practices that have helped me navigate this territory, honoring the past while building something new.

Notice Where Guilt Shows Up Around Rest.

That's the inherited pattern speaking. When you feel guilty for taking a break, pause and ask: *Whose voice is that? Is this guilt based on your actual values, or is it an echo of someone else's survival story?* Recognizing the difference is the first step toward choosing differently. The guilt doesn't mean you're doing something wrong. *It means you're doing something your nervous system hasn't learned is safe yet.*

Practice Rest as Sacred, Honour It.

Choosing to rest in a culture and family system that glorifies exhaustion is a profound act of self-love. Rest not because you've earned it or finished everything, rest because you deserve it. Rest is a biological necessity, not a luxury. Your body needs it. Your mind needs it. Your relationships require you to be rested and refreshed. Reframe rest from *"being lazy"* to *"being loving to yourself."*

Separate Worth From Productivity.

You are not what you produce. Your value isn't measured by output. You are worthy because you exist, because you're human, and because you matter regardless of what you accomplish today. This is perhaps the hardest pattern to break because it feels true in your DNA. Start small. Notice the moments when your worth feels tied to achievement. *Question that.* Practice just being, without doing, and notice how you still matter. *You are still amazing, even when you rest.*

Let Joy Be Ordinary, Not Earned.

You don't need to finish everything first. Joy isn't a reward for suffering or a prize for completing your to-do list. Joy is fuel for living. It's permission to be fully human. It's available right now, in this ordinary moment, if you'll stop long enough to notice it. Eat dessert. Watch the sunset. Laugh with your kids. You don't have to earn those moments. *They're part of a life well-lived, not a prize for a life perfectly executed.*

Model What You Wish You'd Seen.

Your kids or the people you influence are watching. They're learning not from what you say but from how you live. Show them thriving, not *just* surviving. Let them see you rest without guilt. Let them see you choose joy. Let them see you say no to things that don't serve you. They need permission more than they need perfection. *Give them the model you wish you'd had.*

Honour the Past Without Being Bound By It.

Gratitude for what your parents taught you doesn't mean repeating all their patterns. You can love them deeply and still choose differently. You can respect their survival skills and still claim your right to thrive. Take what serves you. Release what doesn't. This isn't betrayal. This is evolution. This is exactly what they would want if they could see clearly: *for you to advance beyond their foundation, not merely maintain it.*

Name the Patterns You're Breaking.

Say it out loud: *"I'm choosing differently. Not because they were wrong, but because I can build on what they started. I'm choosing to rest. I'm choosing joy. I'm choosing to measure my worth by who I am, not what I produce."* Naming the pattern takes away some of its power. This shift transforms the pattern from being an unconscious inheritance into a conscious choice. *You're not just living out a script anymore. You're writing your own.*

Give Yourself the Permission You Didn't Get.

You're allowed to rest. To enjoy. To stop. To say *"this is enough."* You don't need anyone's approval for that. Not your parents', not society's. Not even your own inner critic. Give yourself permission. You're the only one who can. You're the only one who needs to. The permission you give yourself today is the permission your children will learn from watching you. *Make it generous.*

What Gets Passed Forward.

When I look at my kids now, I see them navigating their own balance between the resilience I taught them and the permission I'm learning to give them. They work hard because they've watched me work hard. They also rest without guilt because they've watched me learn to do that, however imperfectly. They push themselves toward goals because they've inherited that drive. They also know when *enough is enough* because I'm teaching them what I'm still learning.

That's the gift we can give the next generation: both the strength to endure and the wisdom to enjoy. This includes both the capacity to build and the permission to rest in what has already been built. It was our resilience that got us here, it is our thriving that makes being here worthwhile. We're not rejecting what came before us. We're completing the circle of growth and allowing the expansion of ideas to occur. We're showing that *survival and thriving aren't opposites.* They're partners and both necessary for a full life.

Take the strength you have inherited and add your softness. Take the determination you know you have and add in self-care and intentional relaxation. Take the resilience you have built in yourself and add the joy you deserve. That's growth. *That's gratitude in action.* That's building on the foundation they laid, taking it one layer higher. Let them see how their hard work made your life fuller and your dreams possible.

They survived so you could thrive. Honour that by actually thriving. By living the life they couldn't quite imagine. By showing your children what's possible when strength meets permission, when resilience meets rest, and when survival becomes the foundation for something even grander.

Thrive Principle: Generational Thriving

You can honour your parents' resilience while choosing patterns they couldn't model. Take their strength. Add your rest. That's not rejection, it's completion. They survived so you could thrive.

CHAPTER FIFTEEN

Living with Purpose & Meaning

Truth Be Told

When I was young, my purpose felt clear and simple. Get an education. Build a career. Prove I could make something of myself. The path felt linear, the destination visible. I knew what I was working toward because *the world had shown me what success looked like.*

Then I married, had a family, and my priorities shifted overnight. Purpose became about them. About creating a stable home, raising good kids, working full-time, and supporting my husband's dreams alongside my own. My days were filled with the beautiful, exhausting work of building a life together. Purpose lived in the ordinary rhythms: school lunches, family dinners, and the thousands of small moments that create a childhood, marriage, and *home.*

After I went into the shelter, everything collapsed. In that moment, purpose distilled to pure survival. *Keep myself safe. Find a place to live. Prove I could make it. Get through one day, then the next, then the next.* There was no room for philosophical questions about meaning. There was only the raw necessity of rebuilding from nothing.

Coming out of that season, something shifted in my understanding of purpose. It wasn't about grand achievements or proving myself. It wasn't about *what looked impressive from the outside.* Purpose served as my North Star, the thing I navigated myself, when everything else felt dark. When questions lingered and I wasn't clear, I brought my purpose to the forefront to be my shining light. Dad invited me to come work in his office for a brief time, to earn money, to start fresh, and to get back on my feet. He said it would take my mind off things.

As my purpose became my beacon, my life began to shift. I remarried seven years later. I found respect, a genuine partnership, and a *connection I didn't know was possible.* I discovered peace in ways I'd never experienced. I could practice my faith freely. Harmony blossomed between who I was and how I was living. A deeper love for life came after nearly losing it. I fully understood how precious and fragile our happiness is.

What once was about doing, achieving, proving, and providing is now about something quieter and deeper. *My focus now shifts to finding purpose and meaning.* Living in a way that reflects what I've learned, what I value, and what I want to leave behind. *The goals that motivated me at twenty-five don't drive me now.* The purpose that gave structure to my thirties doesn't quite fit who I have become. That's growth. That's exactly what's supposed to happen when you find the meaning in what truly matters most.

Dad's Purpose Evolution

Watching Dad's purpose transform across his lifetime taught me this truth long before I had language for it. Young Dad's purpose was survival and provision. His primary focus was keeping the family fed and providing a roof overhead. Building security out of nothing. That singular focus drove him through impossibly hard years by giving him the strength to push through exhaustion and setbacks. His determination to survive transformed him into a man who never quit.

Middle-aged Dad's purpose expanded. Grow the business. Raise the family. Serve the community. Build something that lasts. Create opportunities for others. I watched as his circle widened, his impact deepened, and his sense of what mattered included more than getting by. He was building a legacy, though he would never have called it that. He was building something that held more meaning and fueled his purpose to carry on.

Later, Dad's purpose shifted again, especially after his heart attack forced him to slow down. Even though cutting back was all new, it worked for him, because using naps, Dad eventually went on to continue working into *his early nineties.*

Those porch evenings I've mentioned weren't aimless. Their purpose was redefined in a more gentle manner. Being present became as important as being productive. Enjoying what he'd built mattered just as much as the building he'd done. Mentoring the next generation, loving his grandchildren, passing on wisdom in quiet conversations, these became the work that mattered to him, and carried the meaning he wanted to invest in.

Near the end, Dad's purpose distilled to something even simpler. Love well. Let go gracefully. Trust that what he'd built would continue without him needing to control it. He found his inner peace. Each phase honoured what came before while opening him up to what the next season required. He held true to his self's values when he learned to rest. He fulfilled so many dreams and achieved the things that mattered most. Dad showed me that the purpose isn't static. It grows with you. It deepens as you deepen. It changes as life transforms you.

What This Season Is Teaching Me

Right now, I've entered a season where I let go of old ways of operating and I am not actively shaping and forming new rhythms for my life. The structures that once gave my days shape look different now. The work that once defined my purpose has shifted. Some mornings, I wake up wondering what I'm working toward now and what gives this particular season its meaning.

A close friend and mentor, someone whose wisdom has guided me through many transitions, reminds me regularly to pause and revisit the deeper meaning guiding my journey. She asks questions I need to hear: *What really matters most to you right now? What do you want to grow and protect? What's pulling you forward?* Those questions recalibrate me. They bring me back to what's real beneath all the noise.

She also says something that both challenges and comforts me: "*We place obstacles in your path to make you worthy of the endeavour and to maintain your sharpness and learning capacity. There is no learning without stress, and stress is individualized. The response to anything is individualized.*" What she means is this: the seasons when purpose feels unclear aren't problems to fix. They're invitations to deepen. They're preparing for whatever comes next.

I'm learning that purpose doesn't always announce itself with clarity. Sometimes it whispers. Sometimes it emerges slowly through what draws your attention, what breaks your heart, and what you can't stop thinking about even when you try. Purpose often reveals itself in breadcrumbs before it shows up as a clear destination.

I'm also learning that purpose doesn't always announce itself with clarity. It doesn't require a platform or an audience or external validation. Dad's morning ritual of coffee and newspaper and presence was purposeful. My friend, her faithful support for her aging parents; that's purposeful. The teacher who brings genuine care to each student; that's purposeful. The parent who chooses presence over productivity with their kids; that's purposeful.

Purpose is about alignment more than achievement. It's about your actions reflecting your values, your days expressing what matters most to you, and your life pointing toward what you believe is worth building. Some purposes are lived quietly, in ordinary moments, through small consistent choices that no one applauds but that create meaning anyway.

The Saturday Morning Lesson

I think about those early Saturday mornings with Dad, how he'd sit at the kitchen table with his coffee and newspaper. Mom was humming in the background. Nothing fancy. Nothing anyone would write about. Just ordinary time, unhurried and present. Dad didn't measure wealth in dollars but in memories made and moments shared. He'd look up when I wandered in and say, "*This is the good life.*"

Dad's purpose wasn't tied to closing a big deal, buying something new, or achieving a milestone. No, in those ordinary, unremarkable moments, Dad found purpose. *He was discovering richness in the rhythm of an ordinary Saturday morning, rather than waiting for the big wins to feel successful.* Understanding that a good life isn't always dramatic or exciting. Sometimes it's just coffee, newspaper, *and the people you love nearby.*

Those Saturday mornings shaped how I understand purpose now. It's not about the peaks, the achievements, or the moments worth posting about. It's about the ordinary days you actually live in. The quiet sense that what you're doing matters, even when it's simple. Even when no one sees. Even when it doesn't look impressive from the outside.

Purpose in Transition

Maybe you know this feeling. When something that once gave your life meaning begins to change. When you retire, the kids leave, your health changes, or someone you love needs you differently. When you're invited to release what was and be open to what's emerging. The space between can feel disorienting. It can also become the birthplace of discovery that you didn't know you were looking for.

I've come to see that purpose isn't something you discover once and hold forever. It's something you return to, again and again, each time from a slightly different angle. What gave your life meaning at twenty-five might not be what gives it meaning at forty-five or sixty-five. What mattered before your kids were born shifts after they arrive and shifts again when they leave. What motivated you prior to experiencing loss, illness, or significant life changes transforms you into a new identity as these experiences reshape you.

Evolution isn't a problem. *It's the design.* Purpose grows as you grow. It transforms as you transform. Clinging to an old purpose that no longer fits is like trying to live in a house you've outgrown. You can do it, but you'll feel cramped and confined, constantly bumping into limitations that weren't there before. Sometimes the most purposeful thing you can do is let the old purpose release so something new can emerge.

What Pulls You Forward

In this current season, I'm learning to pay attention to what genuinely pulls me forward. The conversations that energize rather than drain me. The work that feels aligned even when it's challenging. The moments when I lose track of time because I'm so engaged. The places where my unique blend of gifts and experiences seem to matter. Purpose often shows up in those quiet pulls before it announces itself as a clear path.

I notice what breaks my heart. What I can't stop caring about. What injustice or suffering or need pulls at me even when I try to look away. Compassion often points toward purpose. The things that break your heart reveal what you're here to mend, witness, or hold space for. Not every broken heart requires you to fix what's broken. Sometimes your purpose is simply to care, to show up, and to refuse to become numb.

I ask what my particular life has prepared me for. *What have I learned that others need to know? What have I survived that could help someone else survive? What do I see that others miss?* Purpose often lives at the intersection of your gifts and the world's needs, your story and someone else's struggle. The hardest seasons of my life, the ones I wouldn't wish on anyone, have become the foundation for helping others through their own hard seasons. That's the purpose emerging from pain.

Thrive Patterns: Eight Ways to Discover and Live Your Purpose

Living with purpose isn't about one dramatic revelation that changes everything. It's a practice of daily alignment, of consistently choosing what matters most, of letting your life reflect your deepest values. These practices help me navigate this territory, providing guidance both when my purpose is clear and when I'm in the process of learning to trust what is still emerging.

Start With What Draws You.

Purpose often reveals itself in what captures your attention without effort. *What problems do you notice that others overlook? What conversations energize you? What would you do even if no one paid you, even if no one noticed or acknowledged your efforts?* Follow those threads. They're leading you toward meaning you might not have recognized. Your purpose isn't always what you think it should be. *Sometimes it's what keeps showing up uninvited, quietly insisting on your attention until you finally listen.*

Notice What Breaks Your Heart.

Pay attention to what moves you, what you can't stop caring about, and what injustice or suffering or need pulls at you. Compassion is often pointing toward purpose. The things that break your heart reveal what you're here to address, to witness, and to hold space for. *Your purpose might be mending what's broken, or it might be simply refusing to look away, creating space for others to be seen in their struggle.*

Ask What Your Life Has Prepared You For.

Your unique combination of experiences, gifts, struggles, and insights has prepared you for something specific. *What have you learned that others need to know? What have you survived that could help someone else survive? What do you see clearly that others miss?* Purpose often lives at the intersection of your story and someone else's need, your wisdom and another person's struggle.

Let the Purpose Be Simple.

It doesn't have to change the world to change a person's life. Your purpose might be raising kids who feel genuinely loved. It might be creating beauty in your corner of the world. It might involve consistently being present for those who need support. It might be doing ordinary work with extraordinary care. Don't dismiss the quiet purposes. *They're often the ones that matter most to the people whose lives they touch directly.*

Align Your Days With Your Values.

Purpose thrives when your actions reflect what you believe matters. Look at where your time and energy actually go. *Does that align with what you say you care about? If not, what needs to shift?* You can't live purposefully if your days are filled with things that don't reflect your deepest values. Start small. One choice at a time. One day at a time. *Small alignments compound into lives that feel deeply meaningful.*

Trust the Transitions.

When your old purpose no longer fits, trust that's information, not failure. You're not losing your way. You're being invited to expand into something that matches who you're becoming. The discomfort of transition is often the growing pain of becoming someone who can hold a bigger, deeper purpose. Let the old release. Make space for what wants to emerge. The clarity will come. May not arrive *on your timeline, but it eventually comes.*

Serve Something Beyond Yourself.

Purpose expands when it includes others. *What are you building that will outlast you? Who benefits from your growth? What gift are you giving that keeps giving after you're gone?* This isn't about grand legacy. It's about recognizing that your life ripples outward. The way you love your family ripples into how they love theirs. The way you treat strangers ripples into how they treat others. *You're always building something bigger than just your own life.*

Return to Purpose Regularly.

Set aside time, whether daily or weekly or seasonally, to reconnect with what matters most. Ask yourself: *Is what I'm doing still aligned with who I want to be? What needs more attention? What needs to be released?* Purpose isn't a destination you reach once. *It's a direction you keep choosing, keep returning to, and keep guiding you home when you've drifted.*

The Gift of Purposeful Living

When I look at my life now, at the different seasons I've moved through, I see something I couldn't see when I was younger. Purpose isn't something you achieve like a marathon. *It's something you practice, maintain, and cherish.* It's not a peak you climb to once. It's a path you walk daily, with intention, attention, and the willingness to adjust when the terrain shifts.

Some days I feel clear and aligned, like every choice is pointing toward something meaningful. Other days I'm just moving through the hours, trying to stay present, trusting that clarity will return when I need it. Both are part of the practice and necessary for a life that sustains itself over decades, not just months.

What I've learned and want to share with you is that purpose does not revolve around having all the answers. It's about living through the questions with integrity. It's about letting your life be guided by what you genuinely care about, not what you *think* you should care about. It's about letting go. It's about building something that reflects your values, whether that something is a career, a family, a community, a body of work, or simply a way of being in the world that leaves it slightly better than you found it.

Dad taught me this in the end, though I'm not sure he knew he was teaching it. His final purposes, to love well and let go gracefully, weren't less important than his earlier purposes of survival and provision. They were the culmination. They were what all the earlier purposes had been building toward. A life where he could finally rest in what he'd created, trust what he'd built, and be at peace with both what he'd accomplished and what he was releasing.

That's what I'm learning to do now in my own way. Rest in what I've built. Trust that my purpose continues to unfold. Be at peace with both the clarity and the uncertainty life offers. Let each season teach me what I need to know for whatever comes next.

If the purpose is the map, hope is the fuel. Hope is essential for survival, while purpose provides direction, a reason to get out of bed, and a means to align our actions with our values. But even survival requires a forward movement and that movement is powered by hope, the quiet belief that *tomorrow can be different than today.*

Hope differs from blind optimism, and it acknowledges problems, too. Instead, hope is an active choice, a decision to keep investing energy in the future, even when the present seems unbearable. Hope allows purpose to survive in the dark.

Sometimes we may feel that keeping hope alive is too difficult, but even the smallest light can burn in our hearts and sustain us. Any kind of light you can see daily can be a reminder of hope. Breathe into hope and release worry and doubt. Feel the steady rhythm of your heart, a quiet reminder that you are alive, that each movement is a new beginning. Imagine a small glowing light within your heart. This is the light of hope. No matter how dim it may seem at times, it is always quietly there, *quietly shining.*

Doubts and darkness may get in the way of seeing that light, creating a barrier, but it is always there, waiting. It is one of life's blessings and mysteries. Imagine this light growing warmer, brighter, and stronger, as if being fanned into glowing embers. See it expanding, filling your entire chest, radiating warmth and comfort.

Hope is not about knowing what the future holds; it's about trusting that even in the darkness, light will return. Even in uncertainty, new possibilities can emerge. Hope is always with you. Even in the darkest moments, light is waiting to return. Carry hope in your heart and share it with the world. Let the warm light of hope expand beyond you like ripples on a pond and touch everyone who needs it so they may see and feel it warming their minds and hearts in its glow. Know that just as you send hope out into the world, you are also receiving it from countless others. Hope connects us all, and everyone is in a state of change. Because nothing remains static and unchanging, hope can create opportunities for newness and miracles to emerge.

In times of struggle, purpose often shrinks. When life is easy, our purpose might be building a business or impacting a community. But when a crisis hits, your purpose might be as simple as saying, "*I will make it through this day.* I say with certainty, your purpose is *already in you.* Your purpose has been forming throughout your entire life, shaped by every experience, lesson, and moment of breaking open and rebuilding. You don't have to force it or find it or prove it. Hope and purpose tell you the work matters. When you're struggling to rebuild from nothing, hope and purpose tell you that every small effort is worth it, because the effort leads somewhere better. Hope protects against despair and despair is the surrender of purpose. Hope is the refusal to surrender, reminding us that transitions are temporary. You just have to keep living with intention, keep paying attention to what matters, and keep choosing alignment over achievement.

There is a dynamic relationship between hope, purpose, and survival. Hope and purpose inform your next step. When the purpose is unclear, hope acts as a guiding light, pulling you toward small, positive actions, not requiring a clear reason (purpose), but a steadfast forward (hope). My dad's generation mastered hope. They had certainty that if they put in the relentless work today, the next generation would have a chance tomorrow. Their collective hope and purpose, the belief in a better outcome for their children, became their enduring purpose.

We all need to find hope in difficult times. By choosing hope, we allow our deeper evolving purpose to remain alive and intact, ready to expand once the darkness lifts. Hope sustains us through uncertainty, ensuring that our life's direction is never completely lost.

The purpose you're seeking is seeking you! It will find you in the life you live, in the showing up you do, and in the grace you give yourself each day. That's enough. That's always been enough. That's the purpose underneath all the other purposes: *To live fully, love deeply, and trust that your life matters simply because you're living it with care.*

Thrive Principle: Living with Purpose & Meaning

Purpose isn't found once and held forever. It's something you return to, again and again, letting it evolve as you evolve. Trust the transitions. Your life is unfolding exactly as it needs to.

CHAPTER SIXTEEN

The Daily Practice of Thriving

You Are Going to Love This

Building resilience isn't a one-time event. Mastering *strength patterns* isn't something you do once and check off your list. If you truly want to wake up one day, look in the mirror, and see a person who's actually thriving continuously, you need to *practice*. Every single day.

That doesn't mean being perfect. I'm not perfect. *Far from it.* There are days I fall back into old patterns, days I react instead of respond, and days I forget everything I've learned and just try to get through. The difference is I now know what brings me back to my centre. I can reconnect to what grounds me. I respect my practices because when I return to them, they help me to become the person I want to be.

I'll admit I have given you lots to think about in these many chapters and even more to implement into your life. When you began this journey with me, I said up front it wasn't going to be easy, but I did tell you it would be *great*. As we come closer to the end, I want to give you one more pivotal suggestion: if you want the life you desire, you are going to need to commit to it with practice.

Practice isn't about adding more to your already full life. It's about understanding that thriving is built upon daily choices and small moments of intentional living that compound over time. 'Practice' versus 'must' is fundamentally different. Practice isn't the goal you push yourself to do. They're the path you take because you want to. They're how you get from knowing what matters to actually living with excitement and desire.

The practices I'm about to share aren't complicated. They're simple. Almost too simple. This simplicity encourages you to attempt each one. Complexity doesn't sustain itself. Simple practices, repeated daily, create lasting transformation. Grand gestures can easily fade. Small, consistent actions compound into a life that looks nothing like where you started. Think about it like building physical strength. You don't go to the gym once and expect to be fit. You don't lift weights for a week and wonder why you're not seeing results. You understand that strength is built through *consistent* repetition, through showing up again and again, through the daily practice of using your muscles until they adapt and grow stronger.

Thriving works the same way. You're building emotional strength, mental resilience, and deep spiritual depth. You're training your nervous system to respond differently than the way it used to. You're creating new neural pathways that make healthier choices feel more natural to you. Ultimately, you're practicing your way into becoming someone who doesn't think life is about surviving, but knows that life is about succeeding each and every day.

Dad's Daily Commitment

Even when Dad didn't have to maintain any particular work schedule, he still showed up to maintain his practices. Every single day he'd wake up at six-thirty. Ride his exercise bike. Have breakfast. Drink his green tea. Read his newspaper and relish in the quiet time before the world woke up and made its demands. He would go to daily mass and then off to his beloved office. He didn't keep that practice because he had to. He practiced this routine because he understood that to remain true to who he was, he needed to start his day in that way. His routine and commitment were ingrained in every fibre of his being.

That's what daily practice looks like. Going beyond simply scheduling self-care into your schedule when available. It is about balance and making your well-being the most important thing and *building everything else around it.* Dad lived decades longer than anyone expected, not because he had perfect genetics or got lucky, but because he practiced taking care of himself every single day. That practice saved his life. It also showed me what commitment to yourself looks like.

After my divorce, I realized I was starting every day in reaction mode. Everyone needs things. Demands were coming at me before I was even fully awake. By the time I had a moment to catch my breath, I was already depleted. I was giving everyone else the best parts of my energy and surviving on whatever was left over.

Finally, with a desire to develop a healthy practice, I started waking twenty minutes earlier. My intention was not to achieve more but to ground myself before giving myself away to the trials of the day. Some mornings it's just coffee in silence. Other mornings it was me journaling my aspirations or meditating quietly. Many mornings it was just sitting with the sunrise, letting my nervous system wake up gently instead of jolting into survival mode.

That twenty minutes changed everything. Not because the time itself was magical, but because starting from centre meant *I moved through the rest of the day differently.* With more intention. Being more present. I prized that time in silence so I could be more capable of responding to challenges instead of reacting to them. That simple practice of twenty minutes allowed me to become the person I knew I could be.

When I skip my practice, I notice immediately. The day feels harder. I was more reactive, more scattered, and more likely to snap at people or make decisions I'd regret. That committed action taught me something crucial: *that practices aren't optional extras.* They're necessary to maintain your intuition and the life you have created after you have built yourself up.

The best news is everyone can find twenty minutes in their day to allocate to practices that support their betterment. It doesn't cost anything and that time certainly pays off. I encourage you to adopt this practice in your life and watch how much it changes you. Over time you will feel the difference and before you know it, those twenty minutes will be non-negotiable, and you'll find the time to do it consistently every day.

What Practices Actually Work

I've tried a lot of practices over the years. Some practices were effective and stuck and I continued with them; some did not. I've learned a few things about what makes a practice sustainable versus what *sounds good in theory* but fails in real life.

First, it has to be simple. If your practice requires perfect conditions, special equipment, or an hour of uninterrupted time, you won't do it. Life *is* messy. Conditions are rarely perfect. The practices that last are the ones you can do when you feel worn out, stressed, and in whatever space you have available.

Second, it has to matter to you. Not to your friend who swears by it. Not to the expert who says you should. To you. If a practice doesn't connect to your values, if it doesn't make you feel more like yourself, if it's just something you think you're supposed to do, you won't sustain it. Find what actually serves you, not what looks impressive.

Third, it has to be flexible. Life changes. Seasons shift. What worked when your kids were little *might not work in your golden years*. What served you before a major loss might *need to be adapted after a big win*. Give yourself permission to evolve your practices as you evolve. Rigid adherence to practices that no longer fit is just another form of disconnection from yourself.

Dad showed me this through his daily commitment to practices that kept him strong, healthy, and present for decades longer than seemed possible. He didn't wait for inspiration. He didn't practice only when he felt like it. He practiced because he understood that who you become is determined by what you do daily, not occasionally. And he loved when they were simple and easy to execute.

The Nightly Practice

One of Dad's most treasured practices was, "*Never go to bed angry.*" He and Mom would kiss goodnight every single night, no matter what had happened during the day. It was their practice of closure, their daily choice to prioritize connection over being right, and their way of preventing small irritations from hardening into permanent resentment.

I adapted that into my own nightly practice. Before bed, I take three minutes to complete the day. *What went well? What challenged me? What am I grateful for? What do I need to release before sleep?* Sometimes I write it down. Sometimes I just think through it. The specifics don't matter as much as the intention to refuse to carry the struggles of today into tomorrow. I gave myself closure. I acknowledged what happened and then *let it go* so I could move on and start the next day fresh.

That simple practice has probably saved me from hundreds of sleepless nights spent rehashing conversations, replaying mistakes, or worrying about things I can't control. It's taught me that completion is a practice, not something that happens automatically. You have to choose it, and you have to create the space for it to happen. Most importantly, you have to honour it before moving onto something else.

Practice During Crisis

I've learned that daily practice isn't about adding more to your life. It's about protecting what matters most. It's crucial to have strong anchors during challenging times. It's about knowing how to return to yourself when you've been pulled in a thousand directions by demands, by grief, by fear, and by the sheer weight of being human and facing things you never expected to face.

During the hardest seasons, my practices simplified. Twenty minutes became five minutes, and five minutes became two deep breaths. That was all I could do, and it mattered because it was still practice. The goal isn't perfection or maintaining some ideal routine no matter what. The goal is staying connected to yourself, to what grounds you, and to the person you're becoming even when everything feels like it's falling apart.

When Dad's dementia started, when my husband had his health scare, and when life threw curveballs that shattered my sense of control, my practices became even more important. Not less. More. Because a crisis doesn't pause to let you get your life together. Crisis demands everything from you. And if you don't have practices grounding you, the crisis will consume you.

Commit to You

If you take one thing from this book, let it be your commitment to yourself. Not in a selfish way, but in a sacred way. Commit to your personal growth. Embrace your inner light. To your becoming. Everything else you want to build, every relationship you want to nurture, and every dream you want to pursue, all of it depends on you showing up as the fullest, most grounded version of yourself.

Committing to yourself is essential. It's recognizing that you are the soil everything else grows from. If that soil is depleted, nothing thrives. If that soil is nourished, everything flourishes. When you commit to your well-being, to your growth, and to your daily practices that keep you grounded and strong, you're not taking away from others. You're ensuring you have something real to give.

Dad understood this intuitively. His morning quiet time wasn't him being self-indulgent. It was him making sure he showed up to the rest of his day as someone calm, present, and capable. His daily nap after his heart attack wasn't laziness. It was him honouring what his body needed so he could keep showing up for the people and work that mattered to him. He committed to himself first, which allowed him to commit to everything else more fully.

That's what I'm asking you to do now. I am not asking you to add more responsibilities to your already overwhelming to-do list. Recognize that the practices you commit to are the foundation that makes everything else possible. They're how you become someone who can handle whatever life delivers. They're how you wake up one day and recognize the thriving person looking back at you in the mirror and feel a sense of pride.

Practices are invitations to elevate our lives. They're the ingredients your body, mind, and spirit need to stay resilient. We commit to what resonates with us and adapt what needs to be changed. Let your practices become your way of honouring yourself, of staying connected to who you're becoming, and of committing to your own thriving life.

Allow me to share some of the favorite practices I have in my life with the hope that it will inspire you to adopt a similar practice in your life.

Move Your Body, Release Your Stress

Your body holds everything, every stress you didn't process, every emotion you pushed down, and every tension you carried through your day. If you never move, all of that stays stuck. Your body needs motion to release what it's holding, to shift energy that's become stagnant, to remember it's alive and capable.

I'm not talking about punishing workouts or forcing yourself to exercise when you hate it. I'm talking about intentional movement that feels good. That reconnects you with your physical self and reminds you your body isn't just a vehicle carrying your brain around but a wise, feeling extension of who you are.

Some days I walk. Some days I stretch. Some days I dance in my kitchen while making breakfast, looking ridiculous and not caring because movement is shifting something in me that was stuck. Your body is trying to help you. It's trying to process, to release, to return to equilibrium. Movement is how you help it do that.

Create Space Between Stimulus and Response

There's a precious moment between something happening and your reaction to it. Most of us live so fast that we miss it entirely. Something triggers us, and we're instantly reacting. Whether it's reacting immediately, sending an email, or saying something we'll later regret, the pause is crucial. We're on autopilot, repeating patterns we don't want, being people we don't recognize.

The pause is where your power lives. In that space between what happens and how you respond, you have a choice. You can react to old patterns, or you can respond to who you're becoming. The pause creates that choice. Without it, you're just running old programs. With it, you're actively shaping who you are.

I practice this constantly. Someone says something that would normally trigger me, and instead of immediately reacting, I pause. I breathe. I feel the reaction rising in me and I just... wait. Sometimes it's two seconds. Sometimes it's walking away for five minutes. In that space, I can choose. *Do I want to react from my wounded places or respond from my strength? Do I want to be right, or do I want to stay connected? Do I want to prove my point, or do I want peace?*

The pause isn't about suppressing your feelings. It's about creating space for wisdom, for choice, for the version of yourself you're trying to become instead of the version old patterns keep pulling you back to. Practice the pause. Before you react, *breathe.* Before you respond, check in with yourself. Before you let autopilot take over, remember you have a choice. That pause, practiced daily, will change your life. It's changed mine.

Protect Your Rest Like Your Life Depends On It

I have mentioned this before in chapter ten. Your life, your health, and your capacity to show up for anything that matters, all of it depends on rest. Real rest. Protected rest. Rest that isn't squeezed into whatever margins are left after you've given everything away.

For years, I treated sleep like an inconvenience, something that got in the way of productivity. I'd stay up late finishing things, wake up early to get ahead, and push through exhaustion because I thought that's what strong people did. What I discovered was that without adequate rest, I wasn't strong. I was barely functioning. I was irritable and scattered, and unable to think clearly or respond calmly. I was surviving on fumes and wondering why everything felt so hard.

Now I will protect my rest. I turn off screens an hour before bed. I create an environment that signals to my body it's safe to let go and relax. I honour the hours of sleep my body needs instead of treating them like a negotiation. Rest is recognizing that you're a human being with a body that needs restoration, not a machine that should run constantly.

Be Where You Are, All the Way

Presence is my favourite. It is the practice of *being all in*, not scattered across a dozen things simultaneously. Too often, we are trying to be everywhere at once and we don't do anything well. I had to learn to stop 'half-doing' everything because I was trying to do too much. Being physically present is crucial, as it prevents your mind from straying three steps ahead or lingering two days behind.

When you're with your loved ones, be with them. Not on your phone. Not mentally running through your to-do list. *With them*. Seeing them. Hearing them. Noticing who they are and the value they bring to your life. Remember the chapter on connections, that is a practice of utmost importance. Being one hundred percent present is the greatest gift you can give anyone, including yourself. When you're working, work. When you're resting, rest. When you're eating, taste your food. When you're talking to someone you love, actually listen instead of planning what you'll say next.

Practice being where you are. Notice when your mind wanders. Gently bring it back no matter how many times you must repeat. This is perhaps the hardest practice because our culture rewards busyness, celebrates multitasking, and makes us feel guilty for doing one thing at a time. Stop yourself regardless. Be where you are, all the way. That's where life actually prospers. That's where connection blooms into something radiant. That's where you begin to live an active and productive life, fully loving life and everything it brings.

Train Your Brain to Notice Good

Science suggests that the brain is wired to spot problems and detect threats and remain alert for dangers. It is constantly thinking of things that could go wrong. That's our survival instinct, and it kept us alive. It also means your default is to scan for what's wrong, what's missing, and what needs fixing. It is constantly looking at the worst-case scenario even if you are not aware of it. Without intentional practice, you'll miss most of the good in your life because your brain isn't looking for it. It is focused on surviving. You have to actively teach and train it to see the good, the great, and the glorious that is around you every day.

Gratitude is how you teach your brain to look at the positive in your life. Practicing gratitude isn't about pretending problems don't exist. It's about training your attention to notice good as quickly as it spots problems. Every day, notice three specific things you're grateful for. Not just 'my family' or 'my health.' Specific moments. The sunrise was spectacular. The friend who gave you a hug at the perfect time. The sound of a bird chirping outside your window or your ability to persevere through a challenging day are moments to cherish. These are things to be grateful for and when you train your brain to notice them, will automatically begin to recognize similar positive details more often.

Seeing the good around you will rewire your brain over time. You start noticing pleasant things automatically instead of only when you're deliberately looking for them. You become someone who sees abundance alongside struggle, beauty alongside hardship, and reasons to keep going alongside reasons to give up. This doesn't make the hard things disappear. It makes them bearable. It reminds you that even in difficult times, there are moments worth savouring, and being grateful for.

However you practice gratitude, make it daily, specific, and genuine. Let your appreciation shift how you see your life, how you move through your days, and how you meet challenges and prevail. Gratitude doesn't change your circumstances. It changes how you see them and react. And when you change that, everything else shifts with it.

Step Forward with Grace

As you learn these practices and implement them into your life, be kind to yourself when you forget. There might be days when you skip practices or justify not doing them. You'll get too busy. You may lose motivation or convince yourself it doesn't matter. Then you'll remember. And when you do, I need you to return to them with kindness and grace. Just return to the practices and recommit. Don't wait, do it right then. This is the crucial moment. Start again. That's the practice. It's not about never falling off, but about *always getting back on track.*

I've fallen off these practices more times than I can count. I've gone weeks without my morning grounding, skipped my nightly routine completely for months, and let my rest become something I squeeze in around everything else. Every single time, the voice in my head wants to tell me I've failed, *I've ruined my progress, and I might as well give up.* Still, I practice, returning without listening to that voice and doing so with self-love and grace.

The return is where your strength lives. Not in perfect performance, but in your willingness to start again. To say, "*I'm human. I drifted. Now I'm returning.*" No drama or shame involved. Just the quiet commitment to myself, to my practices, to the person I am becoming through daily, imperfect effort. If you fall off, remember you haven't failed. You've just been reminded that you're human. Jump right back in. Now you get to return to your practice and prevail. That is the real practice, coming back again and again, without judgment toward yourself. That might be the most important practice of all, teaching you that perfection isn't the goal. Returning is. Showing up for yourself, again and again, no matter how many times you drift away.

Your Commitment to Yourself

I encourage you to start with just one practice and build from there. Whichever one called to you most strongly, pick that one. Practice it tomorrow. Then repeat the process the following day. Then the next. Let it become part of who you are.

Then, when you're ready, add another practice. Build it slowly. Create in a way that is sustainable for you. Build in a way that honours your real life, the things you value, and the goals you wish to achieve. That commitment, practiced daily, will change everything.

It won't happen overnight, but it will happen steadily, certainly, and undeniably. One day you'll wake up and realize you've become who you've been working towards and everything you built is thriving all around you.

You deserve this attention to yourself and your own self-care. Your daily commitment going forward should be about becoming someone who fully thrives in life. Our body is our inner teacher. Making that commitment starts today. Don't wait for everything to settle down or until you've earned it through enough turmoil. Now. *This very moment.* By repeating these simple practices daily, you will catapult yourself into a completely different life.

Commit to yourself.

You're totally worth it.

Thrive Principle: The Daily Practice of Thriving

Thriving is built through daily practice, not occasional effort. Small actions, repeated consistently, compound into lives that look nothing like where you started. Practice daily. Return often. Become who you're meant to be.

PART 3:

REFLECTION & APPLICATION

The Life You Build Through Daily Practice

You've made significant progress, my friend. You've come a long way. You've learned the principles of building a resilient foundation and you've seen examples of what it truly means to thrive. You've read stories from my life and my father's lives, understood concepts about strength, survival, and growth, and hopefully found pieces of yourself reflected in these pages.

Now comes the real work. Not reading about thriving, but actually living it. Up until now, I've been sharing my journey, my father's wisdom, the lessons I've learned through building and falling apart and rebuilding again. But this next part isn't about me anymore. This part is about you. Your story. Your patterns. Your practices. Your blueprint for the life you want to build. Everything up to this point has been preparation, laying the groundwork so you'd have the principles and examples you need. Now you get to take all of that and make it uniquely yours.

These final chapters will give you space to reflect honestly on where you are right now and to assess what's working in your life and what isn't. I want to provide a place for you to identify the patterns you've been repeating without realizing it. This is how you recognise the resilience you've already built. I want to give you a sacred place to design the practices and systems that will fit into your life and benefit from them.

As you move into this section, give yourself permission to be imperfect, to not have all the answers and to discover things about yourself you didn't know. Allow yourself permission to go slowly, to take breaks, and to come back when you're ready and recharged. Empower yourself to do this work in whatever way serves you best.

Your blueprint is waiting to be designed. The life you want to build is waiting for you to claim it, not someday when you're finally ready or finally perfect or finally have it all figured out, but right now, together.

Your future self is counting on it, so turn the page. It's time for your life to materialize.

CHAPTER SEVENTEEN

Your Resilience Reflections

Noticing YOU

When I first started doing resilience work in my own life, it was a struggle. I didn't have a roadmap or a manual telling me how to rebuild after everything fell apart. What I did have was what I'd seen, what I'd learned, and the wisdom I'd gained from my father and his example. In the beginning of this book, I spoke about generational wisdom and lessons passed down from others, and how we can learn from their trials and use that knowledge to help us with our own. Now I want to ensure this wisdom gets passed onto you.

Decades of life experiences have shaped who I am, and at this stage in my life, I feel a deep desire to share what I've discovered so it lives on. My hope is that through the gifts passed down by my father, I can equip you with the lessons that will fortify your life and move you forward with grace, self-care, and dignity. I likely benefited from more intentional wisdom-passing than you did. But through this book and this section, together we can discover the resilience and wisdom that's already in you and begin to create the practices and habits you can emulate for someone else.

Imagine a world where more wisdom, care, and life lessons are shared freely, where people support and guide one another toward greater expansion in all our lives. This is the essence of this book: to learn from one another and to pass on what works. Not because we have it all figured out, but because we've walked through fire and come out knowing more about how to build a life we actually adore.

Yes, *adore*. A life you are so in love with and appreciate that you want others to feel the way you do, and you're willing to be the example of how to reach it. That was my desire, to take what I have learned and pass it on so that others could feel more enjoyment in their lives. When I marinated on the concept and the book, I reflected on what made the most difference in my life, and it was the constant teaching from my father about self-resilience.

Now it is time for you to discover the resilience that lives in you.

What I Learned About Resilience

I didn't always know I was building resilience. For years, I thought I was doing life like everyone else. I was getting through the day and doing my best to make it work. I always seemed to be doing what needed to be done despite the hardship. It wasn't until I looked back that I could see the pattern that helped me make it through. Every time I thought I couldn't take another step but took it anyway, I was drawing from my resilience. Every time I fell apart and somehow put myself back together, my resilience showed up.

I was activating the resilience that was inside of me. I didn't know it until I realized the resilience I was using was there all along, I just wasn't utilizing it. I was not tapping into my own reservoir of resilience.

By doing a *self-analysis* and *personal reflection* on what I'd learned from my father, I saw how all that incredible capacity for perseverance and resilience were already a part of me.

That's what this reflection work does. It helps you see what's already there. It gives you language for the strength you've been using by naming it. It shows you that you're not starting from zero. You're starting from a foundation you've possessed all along, brick by brick, choice by choice, step by step, even when you didn't realize what you were activating.

The truth is, you might have been doing the same thing I did, living resiliently, just not drawing from the well. You might not see it yet in action, but it's there. In every challenge you've faced. Evident in every loss you have experienced. In every moment you struggled but persevered. That was your resilience shining through. Not because you did it perfectly or gracefully or without falling apart. Rather, it's because you've persevered, and you're still here. Still trying. Still willing to work hard to ensure the life you have can be different.

Resilience doesn't look the same for everyone, and it doesn't show up the same way in every area of life. Over the years, I've learned that resilience has many faces. Sometimes it's emotional. The ability to feel your feelings without being destroyed by them. The ability to navigate through and process grief, anger, disappointment, and yet still find your way back to hope.

Sometimes resilience is physical. The way your body heals after illness or injury. The discipline to rest when you need rest and move when necessary. The wisdom to listen to what your body is telling you instead of pushing through every signal it sends.

Sometimes resilience is mental and involves the flexibility to adapt your thinking when circumstances change. The strength to reframe challenges as opportunities and the clarity to see patterns and make different choices.

Sometimes resilience shows up in relationships. Resilience often manifests as the ability to endure conflict without losing connection. The courage to repair what's been broken. The grace to forgive, again and again, because connection matters more than being right.

Sometimes resilience is spiritual, involving the ability to find meaning in suffering, the trust that you're part of something larger than yourself, and the peace that comes from aligning your life with what you believe truly matters. This is a crucial aspect of resilience. Sometimes resilience is generational. The wisdom passed down from those who came before, inherited from ancestors who survived impossible things and the knowledge that if they could make it through and overcome, *so can you.*

Finding Your Resilience Reflections

When we take the time to look back and *observe* our life, we quickly see that there are many things we've overcome. We notice when we champion, triumph, and succeed. We see where, against the odds, we used our inner strength and prevailed. If we look at those times, and *reflect* on the circumstances, we can likely say it was using our self-resilience that got us through that test. That reflection helps us see the resilience we already possess.

Resilience Reflections is the practice of looking inward and asking yourself honest questions about how you've been moving through life. Not about judging yourself or finding fault, but about seeing yourself clearly in your greatness. It is when you recognize the patterns that have been shaping your responses and celebrate the strengths you didn't know you had. This isn't complicated work. It doesn't require a therapist or a course or special training. It just requires willingness to be transparent with yourself and self-reflect.

You can do this through journaling, through quiet meditation, through conversations with trusted friends, or simply by paying attention as you move through your days. The specific method matters less than the commitment to notice, ask the inner questions, and gracefully listen to the answers that come.

Resilience Reflections are the intentional, contemplative, mindful practices of looking inward and intentionally pausing to examine how you respond to life's challenges. Reflections invite you to consider your capacity and capabilities to recover, adapt with flexibility, and grow stronger through difficult life experiences. Reflection will allow you to uncover your personal patterns, recognize your strengths, and identify areas where you can continue to grow, while still facing life's inevitable obstacles and hurdles.

Personal reflection is important because the practice transforms daily living into more profound learning. Reflection anchors you, guides you, and helps you thrive, not just survive. Reflection helps you step back and see yourself more clearly. The practice reveals your habits, patterns, beliefs, and emotional triggers, providing you a deeper understanding of why you act or feel the way you do. With self-awareness, you can make conscious choices instead of just reacting.

Resilience Reflections can take shape either as a structured practice or a personal ritual, or both. They may be expressed through journaling about challenging experiences or by engaging with guided, soul-searching questions. Creating intentional space for reflection and asking thought-provoking questions can invite deeper self-awareness within yourself. Try capturing your insights, revelations, and discoveries in writing or recordings so you can observe your growth and progress over time.

Without intentional reflection, we risk falling into cycles, mistaking mere survival for meaningful growth. We end up repeating the same responses that drain us, wondering why our struggles feel so familiar. Life's challenges don't announce themselves or wait for convenient timing. They simply arrive. We need to reflect on life's inevitable challenges. Without reflection, you risk repeating the same draining patterns.

By noticing both your strengths and areas for growth, you build resilience. Over time, *Resilience Reflections* serve as assessment tools and strengthening practices, helping you build a more robust foundation to identify patterns, track growth, and empower yourself to move through life's challenges with reflection and adaptability. Resilience becomes wisdom in the process.

As you work through this chapter, I want to invite you to answer some questions that will help you notice the resilience you already have. These aren't easy questions. Some of them might bring up things you've been avoiding. Some might reveal patterns you'd rather not see. That's the point, to uncover and discover what lives inside of your thoughts and beliefs about yourself. The goal isn't to have perfect answers. The point is to start seeing yourself clearly. To start recognizing what's already there and what you're ready to build next.

Questions to Help You Reflect

Take time right now to be willing to sit with yourself and ask:

How effectively am I managing the current demands and stresses in my life?

_____

_____

_____

_____

Which areas and efforts in my life are currently generating positive results and are working in my life?

_____

_____

_____

_____

What's not? Which systems, practices, or relationships in my life are currently functioning ineffectively?

_____

_____

_____

_____

What do I genuinely need more of right now?

_____

_____

_____

_____

What do I need to actively reduce or eliminate to create more space in my life?

_____

_____

_____

_____

It's wonderful you took the time to reflect on these aspects of your life. They are just the start of learning more about how you see yourself. Trust that what you wrote was right and perfect for this time. Now you can review the answers you gave and change them, improve them, and shift them towards the thriving life you want.

Patterns You're Ready to Shift

Now comes the part where you look honestly at what's not working. Instead of criticizing yourself or listing your mistakes, focus on identifying patterns that you are prepared to change. Awareness is the first step. You can't shift what you haven't acknowledged. So let's acknowledge it with compassion and curiosity instead of judgment.

What patterns do you notice in yourself that no longer serve you? For example, you might engage in people-pleasing until you feel exhausted and resentful, avoid conflict until your relationships deteriorate due to built-up tension, or work yourself into exhaustion in an effort to prove your worth. Perhaps you isolate when things get hard instead of reaching out for support. These patterns made sense once. They protected you or helped you survive. *Now they're limiting what you can build.*

Why are you still operating in survival mode when you're ready to thrive? In what areas might you be concentrating solely on getting through the day, potentially overlooking opportunities to truly enjoy your life? Survival mode saved you. Now it might be holding you back.

I have had to reframe my actions and decisions time and time again when I was annoyed by a friend, argued with my kids, or made decisions that were not conducive to my health. Each time, I used the experience to reframe my behaviour and reset my attitude. The gap between what I know and what I do can be humbling. Some weeks, I'm the picture of intentional living. Other weeks, I'm just getting through, falling back into old patterns I thought I'd moved beyond.

Questions to Help You Reflect

Where am I still operating in survival mode?

_____

_____

_____

_____

_____

_____

_____

What specific thoughts, fears, or limiting beliefs are holding me back?

_____

_____

_____

_____

_____

_____

_____

What is draining my energy and stealing my most valuable time?

_____

_____

_____

_____

What persistent pattern or challenge keeps showing up that I am choosing to ignore or postpone and not deal with?

_____

_____

_____

_____

_____

_____

_____

_____

This is where your focus becomes more fine-tuned. It takes great strength and confidence to face our issues directly and writing them down is the beginning of healing and shifting them. The goal is not to illuminate them completely, but to recognize areas that require more attention and self-acceptance, allowing you to direct your resilience toward them.

Be Kind to Yourself

After years of building and rebuilding my life, I have learned that you don't have to have it all figured out. You don't need to be perfect at being resilient. In fact, you likely get it right every time. But all you have to do is keep reflecting, asking, and digging deeper. Keep trying. Keep choosing yourself and your growth, even when it's hard or especially when it hurts.

Let me remind you, the resilience you're looking for is already in you. It's been there all along, in every moment, you kept going when giving up would have been easier. Each time, you decided to choose hope over despair. In every relationship you fought to repair. Every morning you got out of bed, even though staying there, it felt safer.

You've been building resilience and wisdom your whole life. Now it's time to recognize it. To name it, honour it, and to use it intentionally as you design the life you want foundationally.

The next set of questions will help you do exactly that. But first, take a moment. Breathe. Appreciate how far you've already come. Celebrate the strength that brought you here.

You're ready for what comes next, because this is where you take the time to see your true magnificence. Think about the times in your life when you did something great. Or recall the times you skillfully worked out a problem and forgot to give yourself the credit you deserve. Most of us focus on what we *didn't* do, neglecting the encouraging things we *did* accomplish. I want you to take a moment now to look back and remember your moments of resilience and the times when you prevailed when you forgot to congratulate yourself.

Questions to Help You Reflect

What hard-won wisdom have I already earned through my experiences that I'm currently failing to acknowledge and for which I'm not giving myself credit?

_____

_____

_____

_____

_____

When life knocked me down, how did I get back up and rise again?

_____

_____

_____

_____

_____

What strengths do I have that I've been taking for granted?

_____

_____

_____

_____

_____

What wisdom have I earned through life experience?

_____

_____

_____

_____

_____

Where You're Ready to Grow

I hope answering those questions helped you see the resilience that resides inside of you. And I hope it helped you feel the resilience you can call upon any time you need it.

Resilience Reflection isn't just about looking back and celebrating what you've overcome. It's also about looking forward with intention and clarity. You can see where you are, where you've been, what you've built, and what needs attention, so you can grow. It's not about where you or where others think you should grow, but where you feel the pull toward something more. *Where is the place you experience a genuine desire to expand, evolve, and transform into the new, thriving version of yourself?*

What excites you when you imagine your future? What possibility makes you lean forward with interest instead of pulling back in fear? What version of yourself can you see clearly enough to start building toward? Growth doesn't happen without vision. You need to know what you're building toward, even if the path isn't clear yet. The vision pulls you forward when motivation fades. When everything else feels uncertain, it acts as a beacon and guides you home.

Think about one single area of your life that, if you focused real attention there, would transform everything else. Maybe it's your physical health. Maybe it's a key relationship. Maybe it's your relationship with money, work, or rest. You can't change everything at once, *but if you could choose one area to focus on, knowing that shifting it would create positive ripple effects everywhere else, what would it be?*

The questions below will help you clarify where you're being called to grow. Answer them honestly. Write what comes to mind first, without editing or censoring yourself. There are no wrong answers here. This is about discovering what's true for you right now, in *this* season of your life.

Questions to Help You Reflect

What repeating patterns keep showing up in my life that I'm ready to change?

_____

_____

_____

_____

_____

What nourishment, movement, or rest must I start prioritizing for my body?

_____

_____

_____

_____

_____

What relationships and connections in my life nourish my spirit and truly sustain me?

_____

_____

_____

_____

_____

What hard-won wisdom would I pass on to someone or someone else going through what I've been through?

_____

_____

_____

_____

_____

_____

Where do I feel called to grow and learn next?

_____

_____

_____

_____

_____

Honour these answers and come back to them again and again. You'll be amazed at how wise they are, and over time, you'll see how intuitive they'll become in the direction of where your life is headed next.

The Gift of Reflection

If answering those questions felt inspiring, just know, *Resilience Reflections* are not a one-time exercise. They're an ongoing practice, a way of moving through life with greater awareness and intention. The more consistently you practice looking inward, the clearer your patterns, your strengths, and your path forward will become.

Make reflection a regular part of your life. Maybe it's journaling every morning. Or it's a monthly check-in with yourself. Hopefully, it's pausing after difficult experiences to ask, *"What is this teaching me?"* By looking inward, you can celebrate the strengths you possess while also identifying where you'd like to grow. Balance builds confidence and humility at the same time. Reflection allows you to learn from experience and turn everyday events, both successes and struggles into valuable lessons. You can reduce your future challenges by applying this wisdom and insight gained through consistent reflection.

When life feels easy and more in flow, you can be certain that the reflection you did here helped you reconnect with your more divine self. The practice of reflection helps you align your inner knowing, infinite wisdom, and deeper purpose.

By doing this reflection work, you are now ready to design your ultimate, thriving blueprint. Take everything you just discovered and use it intentionally to create a life that not only excites but also exhilarates you. You've done important work by reflecting on your resilience. You've looked honestly at where you are, what you've survived, what you've built, and where you're ready to grow. This isn't just drafting answers. This is you claiming your future and seeing clearly what you *can* manifest. You are exactly where you need to be, with everything you need, ready to build something beautiful, so say *thank you* to yourself and *yes* to what's next.

CHAPTER EIGHTEEN

Knowing Your Resilience Strengths

Resilience Patterns in You

Now comes the part I've been so excited to share with you. You're about to design something magnificent and entirely yours. A blueprint for a life that not only works but also absolutely thrives. A life that lights you up, and like I said before, *a life you adore.*

Everything you've reflected on, everything you've discovered about your resilience, every pattern you've named and every strength you've recognized, all of that becomes the foundation for what you're creating next. This chapter is about taking all that wisdom and turning it into something tangible and beautiful. Something you can live by that guides your choices and illuminates your days.

Think of this as your architectural plan for thriving and you're the architect. You're the designer, the one deciding what this life looks like, feels like, and becomes. Instead of simply copying someone else's blueprint, create something uniquely and gloriously yours. A blueprint that celebrates your life, honours your real circumstances, and expresses your genuine desires. A blueprint that understands where you've been while pointing you boldly toward the magnificent life waiting for you.

This is where you become intentional about every room you create, every window you open to let light flood in, and every doorway that leads somewhere *new and extraordinary*. You're building something beautiful, sustainable, and entirely your own. And the most wonderful part is you now know how to do it and make it long-lasting and obtainable.

Make a Magnificent Blueprint

A magnificent blueprint isn't rigid or restrictive. It doesn't consist of strict rules that you must follow perfectly, resulting in failure. A magnificent blueprint is a living, breathing document, a guide that helps you make decisions aligned with who you're becoming. It's flexible enough to dance with life's changes, strong enough to keep you grounded when things get chaotic, and clear enough to remind you what matters most when you temporarily lose your way.

Dad used to say that the best buildings are the ones designed with both expansion and flexibility in mind. Secure enough to stand through storms. Flexible enough to expand when the family grows, when dreams get bigger, and when life invites you to become something more. That's what your blueprint gets to be. Rooted in solid principles of resilience but adaptable to every beautiful season life encounters. Your blueprint is *Built to Thrive* and designed to evolve as you do.

Before we start designing your specific blueprint, let's celebrate the different types of resilience you're already working with. Just like a well-built house has diverse systems, electrical bringing power, plumbing bringing water, and structural beams holding everything together, your resilience shows up powerfully in different areas of your life. Understanding these different types helps you see where you're already remarkably strong and where you have valuable opportunities to grow.

Different Types of Resilience

What I've come to discover and absolutely love is that resilience isn't one thing. It's a kaleidoscope of beautiful, multi-faceted gifts that shows up in different areas of life and expresses itself differently according to each situation and what's needed. Understanding these different types can help you celebrate where you're already thriving and get excited about where you're ready to expand.

I want to outline each resilient type because we all go through them and not a day goes by when one isn't called to the forefront to help us out. They also show that we are not one-dimensional, we have many areas of life that need our resilience and different parts of our life require different expertise. As you read the different types of resilience, see where in your life these show up and how your positive resilient patterns can assist.

Emotional Resilience:
Your Inner Strength

Emotional resilience is your remarkable ability to recover from setbacks, navigate challenges with grace, and protect your well-being during difficult times. It's the capacity to fully experience your emotions without allowing them to consume you or hold you back. This resilience helps you process feelings of grief, anger, and disappointment, so you can still find your way back to hope and joy.

I discovered my emotional resilience while staying at the women's shelter, although I didn't recognize it as such at the time. Those early mornings when I woke up and reality washed over me, I needed all the strength and resilience I could muster. The magnitude of beginning anew is immense. The uncertainty of what came next was overwhelming. I was filled with grief for what I had left behind. I could have let those feelings consume me completely. Instead, I learned to feel them, honour them, sit with them, and then chose to keep moving forward anyway. That's *emotional resilience*. Not pretending everything's fine, but about fully experiencing everything and still choosing hope.

Ask yourself with curiosity:

- *How do I usually respond to stress or obstacles?*
- *Which coping strategies have beautifully supported me in the past?*
- *How do I process and recover from emotional setbacks in ways that honour my feelings while moving me forward?*
- *What helps me regulate my emotions during difficult times?*
- *When have I maintained emotional balance even when facing uncertainty?*

Physical Resilience:
Your Body's Wisdom

Physical resilience is your body's incredible ability to recover from stress, maintain vibrant health, adapt to physical challenges, and sustain energy over time. It's the miraculous way your body heals after illness or injury. Physical resilience is the wisdom and ability to know when to rest when you need rest and when to move when you need movement. The deep listening that enables you to hear what your body is telling you instead of overriding every signal it sends.

Dad's heart attack unexpectedly taught our whole family about physical resilience. Before that, he thought his body was invincible. He believed he could work longer and push himself harder without rest, constantly feeling the pressure to do more. His heart had other plans and offered him a powerful gift. After the heart attack, he truly learned to listen. His daily nap wasn't weakness or giving up. It was profound wisdom. It was his body's way of saying, *"I need this to keep serving you well."* And he honoured that.

Consider with appreciation:

- *What are the primary ways my body responds to and recovers from stress?*
- *What physical practices help me build strength and sustained vitality?*
- *What daily practices will help me hear my body's needs and respond with genuine care?*
- *What vital messages is my body trying to tell me that deserve my loving attention?*

Mental Resilience:
Your Adaptable Mind

Mental resilience is your mind's beautiful ability to adapt, process challenges creatively, maintain focus, and recover from mental stress. It's the flexibility to adjust your thinking when circumstances change. The ability and strength to reframe challenges as opportunities for growth. It provides you with the clarity to identify patterns and make decisions that empower you.

I watched Dad demonstrate mental resilience every time a business deal shifted or plans didn't unfold the way he'd hoped. He'd pause, think it through from multiple angles, and find another approach. Another possibility. He would often discover an alternative path that proved to be more effective than the initial plan, and didn't get stuck in *"this is the only way"* thinking. He stayed flexible, creative, and solution-focused. He adapted. He found opportunities where others saw only obstacles.

Reflect on with excitement:

- *How do I reframe challenging situations into learning opportunities?*
- *What thought patterns help me stay focused and creative during challenges?*
- *How do I maintain clear-headedness under pressure?*
- *When have I adapted my thinking in ways that opened up new possibilities?*

Social Resilience:
Your Connection Strength

Social resilience is your capacity to maintain, repair, and strengthen meaningful connections while navigating interpersonal challenges. It's patience to weather conflict without disconnecting completely. The courage to repair what's been broken. The grace to forgive, again and again, because connection matters more than being right.

The relationships that sustained me through my most challenging seasons weren't perfect relationships. They were beautifully real ones who showed up and stood up for me, even during my most struggling times. Family members who loved me through my messiest moments. People who stayed when it would have been easier to walk away demonstrate social resilience. That's social resilience in action. Instead of completely avoiding conflict, they skillfully navigated through it without losing the precious connection beneath.

Think about with gratitude:

- *How do my relationships support me through difficult times?*
- *What role do I joyfully play in others' resilience journeys?*
- *How have I rebuilt trust after relationship challenges in ways I'm proud of?*
- *What connections really keep me going and give me energy?*

Spiritual Resilience:
Your Deeper Anchor

Spiritual resilience is your connection to meaning, purpose, transcendence, and the deeper dimensions of existence that sustain you through life's challenges. It's your ability to find meaning even in suffering and trust that you're part of something infinitely larger than yourself. Aligning your life with what you believe is important and truly matters brings you peace.

Dad's faith was his unshakeable anchor. Even when everything else felt uncertain, when business was struggling and when the family faced challenges, he had something solid and eternal to stand on. His faith wasn't just Sunday morning religion. It was beautifully woven into how he lived, how he made decisions, and how he treated every person with dignity. *"If God is with us, who can be against us?"* he'd say with such conviction. That spiritual resilience carried him through decades of magnificent ups and challenging downs.

Ask with openness:

- *What provides my life with a deep meaning during dark periods?*
- *How do I connect with something larger and more enduring than myself?*
- *What practices help me discover peace and purpose?*
- *What anchor holds me steady when everything else shifts?*

Generational Resilience:
Your Inherited Strength

Generational resilience is the strength, wisdom, and adaptive capacity beautifully passed down through families and communities across generations. It's the hard-won wisdom passed down from those who came before you. We inherit this remarkable strength from our ancestors who have overcome seemingly impossible challenges. The empowering knowledge assures you that if they could make it through, so can you.

This is the resilience I've been celebrating throughout this entire book. The powerful lessons Dad learned during his nine decades on this earth and the survival skills his generation mastered. Dad's determination, resourcefulness, and absolute refusal to give up that was passed down to me now lives vibrantly in my children and grandchildren, ensuring this strength ripples ahead. We carry the strength of our ancestors in our bones and their wisdom in our choices. Their resilience is active in our ability to keep going and even thrive when things get hard.

Consider with reverence:

- *What essential survival wisdom has been lovingly passed down in my family?*
- *How can I honour past struggles while intentionally creating exciting new opportunities?*
- *What specific resilience gifts do I want to joyfully pass on to future generations?*
- *What specific strength, courage, or wisdom am I already carrying that I inherited from those courageous ones who came before me?*

Your Unique Resilience Profile

Now that you understand these six powerful types of resilience, take a moment to celebrate your own unique resilience profile. *Where are you naturally and remarkably strong? Where have you developed beautiful resilience through experience? Where do you have exciting opportunities to grow even stronger?*

There's no perfect balance and no scorecard here. You don't need to excel in all six areas to be thriving. Most of us are naturally stronger in some areas than others, and that's not just okay, *it's wonderful*. It makes you uniquely you. The point is to see yourself clearly and lovingly so you can build a life blueprint that amplifies what's already working brilliantly and develops what's ready for your attention.

Questions to Help You Celebrate Your Resilience Profile

Which type of resilience feels most natural and easy for me? Where do I already shine?

Which type have I beautifully developed through experience, even though it didn't come naturally at first?

_____

_____

_____

_____

_____

_____

Which type has exciting potential for growth right now?

_____

_____

_____

_____

_____

_____

Which type, if I strengthened it, would create the most wonderful ripple effects in my life?

_____

_____

_____

_____

_____

_____

What empowering patterns do I notice about how I handle different kinds of challenges?

_____

_____

_____

_____

_____

_____

Take a moment to really look at what you've written. These aren't just answers on a page. This is a map of your resilience and precious evidence of your strength. *This is proof that you've been building something remarkable all along, even when you didn't realize it.*

What you're seeing here is your unique resilience signature, the particular way strength shows up in your life. No one else has this exact combination. No one else has walked your path or developed resilience in precisely the way you have. I want you to honour what you're discovering here. Maybe you're naturally gifted with emotional resilience and can process feelings in ways that amaze the people around you. Perhaps your physical resilience has helped you overcome illnesses or injuries that would have debilitated others. Perhaps your mental flexibility helps you find creative solutions no one else sees. Your relationships might be the bedrock that holds everything else together. And possibly your spiritual connection gives you unshakeable peace. What I do know is, you carry generational wisdom that's been passed down through your family like a precious inheritance.

Whatever combination you've discovered, it's exactly right for you. Now that you see it clearly, you can use it more intentionally to build the life you want. This awareness changes everything. When you know where your resilience lives, you can draw from it consciously. By understanding your natural strengths, you allow yourself to draw on them when things get tough. The point is, when you recognize where you're still growing, you can be patient and compassionate with yourself. Celebrate what you've discovered. Really appreciate it. I hope you can agree you're remarkably resilient in your own unique way, and that resilience has brought you to this moment, ready to build a thriving future in so many ways.

CHAPTER NINETEEN

Building Your Personal Blueprint

Being Your Life Architect

This final chapter is about building your personal blueprint. Instead of copying mine or anyone else's blueprint, focus on creating something that is uniquely yours. A blueprint that fits your actual life, your real circumstances, and your genuine desires. This will be a blueprint that honours where you've been while pointing you toward where you want to go. It will be strong enough to withstand any challenges and flexible enough to grow alongside you as you expand and evolve throughout your life.

Think of this as your architectural plan for thriving. Now you're going to design the structure that sits on that foundation. The rooms you want to live in. The windows that let in light. The doors that open to new possibilities. This is where you become the architect of your own life, building something beautiful, sustainable, and entirely your own.

What Makes a Good Blueprint?

What makes a good blueprint is that it isn't rigid. It's not a strict set of rules you must follow perfectly or else you've failed. A good blueprint is a living document, a guide that helps you make decisions aligned with who you're becoming. It's flexible enough to adapt when life changes, strong enough to keep you grounded when things get chaotic, and clear enough to remind you what matters most when you lose your way.

Your personal blueprint should include three essential elements. First, it needs to reflect your values, what truly matters to you, not what you think should matter or what matters to everyone else. Second, it needs to include practices that actually work for you, not practices that look good on paper but don't fit your real life. Third, it needs to have room for growth, for evolution, for becoming someone you haven't even imagined yet.

My Dad believed the beauty of any enduring structure lies in its precision. Every angle, every proportion, every hidden joint tells a story about intention. A lasting life is built the same way, with care in the details, patience in the planning, and enough space in the design to keep growing. Your blueprint should reflect that artistry: crafted with integrity, flexible in its evolution, and always true to the vision only you can build.

Every architect begins with vision, but the structure only stands when that vision is translated into purpose. A blueprint without meaning is just lines on a page. Before you can build anything lasting, you must decide what gives it heart, what makes it worth constructing in the first place.

Start With What Matters Most

Before you can design anything, you need to know what you're building toward. *What truly matters to you?* It's not about what your parents valued, what society deems important, or what was important five years ago. Focus on what matters to you right now, in this season of your life.

This is where your values come in. Values are the non-negotiables, the things you're not willing to compromise on, and the principles that guide your decisions when everything else feels uncertain. They're the foundation your blueprint rests on. Without clear values, every decision becomes harder than it needs to be. With clear values, choices become simpler because you know what you're building toward.

Take some time right now to identify your core values. *What do you stand for? What do you want your life to be about? What would you regret not prioritizing if you looked back on your life in twenty years?* These aren't just nice ideas. These are the principles that will shape every other decision you make as you build your blueprint.

Questions to Help You Clarify Your Values

What brings me genuine joy and fulfillment?

_____

_____

_____

_____

_____

_____

What would I protect or fight for, no matter what?

_____

_____

_____

_____

_____

_____

What do I want to be known for?

_____

_____

_____

_____

_____

_____

_____

When I'm at my best, what principles am I living by?

_____

_____

_____

_____

_____

_____

What legacy do I want to leave?

_____

_____

_____

_____

_____

_____

Please take a moment to look at what you wrote. These aren't just answers. These are the pillars your blueprint will rest on. Everything else you design needs to support these values. When you're living in alignment with your values, life feels easier, more meaningful, and more true.

Once your values are clear, they become the quiet compass that directs every design choice. Now it's time to translate those values into the rhythm of your days: the habits, rituals, and routines that give your life structure. Just as a foundation supports a building, your daily actions support the person you are becoming.

Design Your Daily Foundation

The rhythm of your days becomes the strength of your life. What you do consistently shapes what you stand on. Choose practices that restore you, not routines that exhaust you. Simple moments of alignment, done with presence, become the bearing walls that hold everything together.

Think about *what* restores you. Not what you think should restore you, but what actually works. For some people, it's movement. For others, it's stillness. For some, it's a connection. For others, it's solitude. There's no right answer here. There's only what's true for you.

Dad's mornings always began with small acts of structure. He'd straighten his workspace, sharpen a pencil, and review his plan for the day. It wasn't about control; it was about clarity. Those few intentional minutes built the framework for everything that followed, reminding him that order starts within before it ever appears around us.

What matters isn't how much time these rituals take, but how consistently they return you to balance. Even a few minutes of presence can shift the entire framework of your day. The goal isn't to create the perfect routine; it's to craft one that keeps you aligned with yourself.

Questions to Help You Design
Your Daily Practices

What time of day am I most available for myself?

_____

_____

_____

_____

_____

_____

What practices have worked for me in the past, even if I've let them go?

_____

_____

_____

_____

_____

What does my body, mind, or spirit need daily to feel grounded?

_____

_____

_____

_____

_____

What's the simplest version of this practice that I could do even on chaotic days?

_____

_____

_____

_____

_____

_____

How will I protect this time from other demands?

_____

_____

_____

_____

_____

Build Your Support Structure

No blueprint stands alone. Every strong structure needs support beams, reinforcements, and connections that hold everything together when pressure builds. In your life, these support structures are your relationships, your community, and the people who help you stay standing when everything else feels unstable.

Look at the relationships in your life right now. *Which relationships genuinely contribute and support your growth? Which ones drain you? Which ones challenge you in ways that make you stronger? Which ones make you feel small?* Your blueprint needs to include the right people, the ones who genuinely want to see you thrive, who celebrate your wins without jealousy, and who sit with you through losses without trying to fix you.

Dad taught me that you can tell who your real construction crew is by who shows up when things fall apart. Not when everything's going well and it's easy to be supportive. However, during times of complexity, life gets messy and complicated, and there's no clear solution. Those are the people you build your life around. Those are the ones who belong in your blueprint.

The strength of any design lies in its connections. The right people act like beams that share the weight and hold the vision steady when you cannot. Choose your crew with care. They help turn your blueprint from theory into reality.

Questions to Help You Build Your Support Structure

Who in my life truly wants to see me thrive?

_____

_____

_____

_____

_____

Which relationships energize me instead of draining me?

_____
_____
_____
_____
_____
_____
_____

Who can I call when things fall apart?

_____
_____
_____
_____
_____
_____
_____

What relationships need better boundaries?

_____
_____
_____
_____
_____
_____
_____

Where do I need more connection, and where do I need more space?

_____

_____

_____

_____

_____

_____

_____

Your blueprint should include intentional decisions about relationships. Not just letting whoever shows up stay in your life, but actively choosing who gets your time, your energy, and your trust. This isn't about being cold or cutting people off. It's about recognizing that your energy is finite and some relationships genuinely help you thrive while others keep you stuck in patterns you're trying to outgrow.

Create Your Growth Plan

A good blueprint includes room for expansion. You're not building something fixed and final. You're building something that can grow with you as you evolve. This means your blueprint needs to include how you'll keep learning, adapting, and becoming someone capable of more than you are today.

What does growth look like for you right now? Maybe it's learning a new skill. Maybe it's healing an old wound. Maybe it's developing a quality you admire in others. Maybe it's simply becoming more consistent with the practices you already know work. Growth doesn't have to be dramatic. It just has to be intentional.

I've learned that the most sustainable growth happens when you focus on one area at a time. Instead of trying to change everything simultaneously, try choosing one meaningful area and giving it real attention. When that becomes solid, you move to the next. This is how you build something lasting instead of burning out trying to change everything at once.

Questions to Help You Create Your Growth Plan

What area of my life, if I focused real attention there, would create the greatest and positive ripple effect?

_____

_____

_____

_____

_____

_____

_____

_____

_____

_____

What skill or quality do I want to develop this year?

_____

_____

_____

_____

_____

_____

_____

What old pattern or wound am I ready to heal?

_____

_____

_____

_____

_____

_____

_____

What does success look like in this area six months from now?

_____

_____

_____

_____

_____

_____

What support or resources do I need to make this growth possible?

_____

_____

_____

_____

_____

Write down one specific growth goal. Ensure it is concrete enough that you'll know if you're making progress. Make it small enough that it feels achievable. Make it meaningful enough that you actually care about it. Then break it down to the smallest possible next step. Don't focus on the entire journey. This week, focus on taking the very first step you can.

Design Your Rest and Renewal

Here's something most of us miss: rest is essential. It's not what you do after everything else is finished. It's part of the foundation. Without rest built into your blueprint, everything else eventually crumbles. Your relationships suffer. Your work suffers. Your health suffers. You suffer.

Your blueprint needs to include how you'll rest, how you'll restore your energy, and how you'll keep yourself from burning out. This means making rest non-negotiable, not something you fit in when there's time left over. This is crucial because time is a finite resource. You have to create time for rest the same way you create time for work.

Dad learned this the hard way when his heart attack forced him to slow down. After that, his daily nap wasn't optional. It was prescribed. It was necessary. It was the thing that kept him alive and thriving for decades longer than most people his same age. He built rest into his daily routine the same way he incorporated work into it. Both mattered. Both were essential.

Questions to Help You Design Your Rest

How much sleep does my body actually need to function well?

_____

_____

_____

_____

_____

_____

_____

What activities genuinely restore my energy instead of just distracting me?

_____

_____

_____

_____

_____

_____

_____

Where in my schedule can I protect time for rest?

_____

_____

_____

_____

_____

What boundaries do I need to set to make rest possible?

_____

_____

_____

_____

_____

What's my signal that I need rest before I hit complete exhaustion?

_____

_____

_____

_____

_____

Include rest in your blueprint as intentionally as you include work. Schedule it. Protect it. Treat it as seriously as any other commitment. This isn't selfish. This is strategic. This is recognizing that you can't build anything sustainable if you're constantly running on empty.

When you rest, you renew the energy that fuels your purpose. The stillness between efforts is where inspiration returns and clarity takes form. From that calm place, you can ask the most important question of all: why you're building in the first place.

Map Your Purpose

Every good blueprint has a purpose. There is a purpose for your existence. Your life blueprint needs the same thing. *What's the purpose of all this building? What are you creating this life for? What do you want your days to be about? What truly matters to you most?* Mapping purpose in your life is the process of deliberately translating your inner beliefs into external actions, ensuring that your daily life is aligned with what you deem most important.

Identify your destination. Determine what gives your life meaning. This could be service, creativity, learning, or financial freedom. Establish a clear vision of the life you want to build and the person you want to become.

Establish your coordinates through your values and principles. Pinpoint your fundamental beliefs like integrity, compassion, or hard work. These are the bedrock of your map. Define the important roles you play, (parent, partner, professional, friend, and citizen) and establish how much time and energy you want to dedicate to each one based on your purpose.

Plot your route through your strategy. Check your current daily activities against your established values. If your purpose is family connection, but you spend ninety percent of your time on work, your map is misaligned. Set goals with intention, and goals are not tasks. They become milestones on the map that move you toward your overall purpose. If your purpose is wellness, then the goal is to exercise three times a week.

Mapping purpose gives you a tool to use in moments of reaction or confusion (as discussed in the "Power of the Pause"). You can pause and ask, "*Does this choice move me closer to my map's destination or further away?*"

Recognize that your map is not static. As your life changes (like Dad's purpose evolving after his heart attack), intentionally review and adjust your map to match who you are becoming, ensuring your actions remain aligned with your deepest, current meaning.

Mapping your life's purpose doesn't have to be grand or require changing the world. It can be as simple as raising kids who feel loved or beautiful in your corner of the world. Showing up faithfully for the people who need you. Being a safe person for others to turn to and rely on. Living intentionally and living with integrity even when no one's watching.

The question isn't whether your purpose is big enough or impressive enough. The question is whether it's true enough. The question is whether your purpose aligns with your true self and the things you genuinely care about. Whether it gives your daily choices meaning beyond just getting through another day.

Mapping purpose transforms your life from a series of random events into an intentional, directional journey.

Questions to Help You Map Your Purpose

What am I naturally drawn to care about?

_____

_____

_____

_____

_____

_____

_____

What breaks my heart in a way that moves me to action?

_____

_____

_____

_____

_____

_____

What would I do even if no one ever noticed or appreciated it?

_____

_____

_____

_____

_____

_____

What impact do I want to have on the people closest to me?

_____

_____

_____

_____

_____

_____

_____

_____

_____

How do I want to feel when I look back on this season of my life?

_____

_____

_____

_____

_____

_____

_____

_____

_____

Your purpose doesn't have to be permanent. It can evolve as you evolve. What matters now might shift in five years. That's okay. That's growth. What matters is that you're living with intention right now, making choices aligned with what feels meaningful to you in this season.

Put It All Together

Now you have all the pieces. Your values. You have established yourself and your daily practices. Your support structure is crucial, as is your growth plan. Prioritize rest and renewal. Your purpose. These aren't separate pieces. They all work together to create your own personal blueprint for thriving.

Take a moment and look at everything you've written in this chapter. All those answers, reflections, and decisions. This is your blueprint. One hundred percent you. All yours. Real. Honest. Built on what you actually know about yourself, not what you think you should be.

The journey to a thriving life moves from awareness to action. Everything in this book and what you've created isn't just a plan, it's a portrait of your inner architecture, a reflection of how your life fits together when you design it with intention. This blueprint is your guide, honouring your past to discover your purpose.

When decisions feel overwhelming, come back to your values. When you're exhausted, focus on your rest plan. Make a stronger commitment to your purpose when you're feeling lost. Be in the company of your people when you need help and support. This blueprint exists to help you make choices aligned with who you're becoming, not who you used to be.

A commitment to self, to continuous growth, self-compassion, and the foundation for the life you are building right now ensures you have something real and sustained to give to the world and to others. Generational shift breaks limiting survival patterns and creates a new legacy of thriving for the next generation. Compassion teaches emotional resilience and self-love, ensuring setbacks don't become surrender.

Map your alignment and regularly assess your time and energy alignment. Choose alignment over achievement. Anchor with hope and remember that in difficult times, hope is the fuel that powers your purpose. Choose the quiet belief that tomorrow can be better than today.

Final Questions to Complete Your Blueprint

Looking at everything I've written, what's the one change I'm most excited to make?

_____

_____

_____

_____

_____

What's the smallest first step I can take this week?

_____

_____

_____

_____

_____

Who should be informed and needs to know about this blueprint to support me in living it?

_____

_____

_____

_____

_____

How will I know if I'm staying aligned with this blueprint?

_____

_____

_____

_____

_____

What will I do when I inevitably fall off track?

_____

_____

_____

_____

_____

Here's the truth about blueprints: they only matter if you actually use them. This isn't just a beautiful document you create and then forget about. This is a living guide you return to again and again. Questions arise when life becomes chaotic. When making decisions feels challenging, it's important to remember your blueprint. This uncertainty occurs when you are unsure about your next steps. That's when you pull out your blueprint and remind yourself what you're building toward.

Living Your Blueprint

Your blueprint will evolve. It *should* evolve. As you grow, as circumstances change and change, and as you learn more about what works and what doesn't, you'll adjust. That's not failure. That's wisdom. That involves creating and building something that can support you through every season of your life, especially beyond just this one.

But for now, you have a starting point. You have clarity. You have direction. You have a blueprint built on your actual values, your real strengths, and your genuine desires. That's significant. *That's everything.* That's the foundation for a life that doesn't just survive but thrives.

You're ready. You have everything you need. You've discovered resilience in the previous chapter. You have created a blueprint for yourself in this chapter. The blueprint represents the wisdom you've earned through living. The strength you've built through surviving. Now comes the final piece. Now it's time to put everything together and fully embrace the life you're building.

CHAPTER TWENTY

The Legacy of Thriving

Self-Commitment

There comes a moment in every journey when you stop to look back and realize just how far you have come. This is that moment. What used to be uncertain is now a solid and steady path under your feet. What once seemed impossible has become the foundation you now stand on. You have successfully weathered storms, rebuilt what was broken, and learned how to design a life that reflects who you are at your core. This legacy of thriving is not in a finished state or about having reached a plateau. It is about a life lived with continuous intention, guided by wisdom that endures and expands across the threads of time.

You know thriving is not a destination you arrive at. It is a living process, one that keeps unfolding as you grow, stretch, and become. Each step you take adds a new layer to your design, shaping the person you are and the life you are creating. The strength you built through hardship does not disappear once you have healed. It becomes the invisible structure that holds you steady when new challenges arise. Thriving means knowing that even when life changes, your capacity to adapt, learn, and rebuild will remain.

When I think of what it means to truly thrive, I think of my father. His hands carried the memory of work. His voice carried the rhythm of reason. His life embodied the quiet strength of example. This was exemplified by a person who built more than just homes; he built trust and stability. He built trust. He built stability. He built faith in what could last. My father never needed anyone to say that his legacy mattered. He knew it. The care he put into every task, every detail, and every relationship became the blueprint for how to live with purpose. He showed me that real leadership begins with example. It is not about titles or authority. It is about honesty, humility, and the courage to build something meaningful even when no one is supporting you.

That is the lesson I hope you carry forward. The blueprint you have designed through these chapters is not just for you. It is for those who will come after you, those who will watch how you navigate this life and quietly learn from your example. You have become the architect of your own growth, which is an ongoing process that makes you a teacher, a leader, and a guide. The way you live your truth will give others permission to live theirs. The strength you show in hard moments will remind others that resilience is possible. The compassion you extend will teach others how to love. Every action you take builds a bridge between what was and what can be.

I hope I have conveyed that thriving is generational. Every choice you make ripples forward, touching lives you may never see. You now pass on what you learned through your way of life, just as you inherited lessons from those before you. Wisdom is never lost. It moves through time like light through glass, refracting differently in each life it touches. Your story becomes part of that light. Your courage becomes part of that illumination. Each generation adds its own colours, its own designs, and its own dreams, but the source remains the same. We are all builders in the lineage of becoming.

Your life's work now is to embody what you have built. It's important to live by what you know. Demonstrating and showing that thriving is possible even in the face of uncertainty. Strive to become the living example of your own teachings. There is no greater way to lead than by living in alignment with your values and letting the results speak for themselves. When people see you choosing kindness over comparison, forgiveness over resentment, and growth over stagnation, they learn without you having to instruct them. People sense your integrity and find it moving. *You become a quiet leader of transformation.*

Leadership does not always happen on a stage or behind a title. It happens in kitchens and classrooms, in conversations and daily choices. It happens when you keep promises to yourself, listen more than you speak, and speak when you extend grace to someone who has not earned it. True leadership is the art of being responsible for your energy and aware of your impact. The way you show up in your life is the way you shape the lives of others. That is how your blueprint becomes a legacy.

The future needs your examples of living your truth. It needs people willing to live with honesty, compassion, and resilience. You don't need to have all the answers. You only need to be real. When you live authentically, you make it easier for others to do the same.

When you forgive yourself, you give others permission to release their shame. When you stay open to learning, you invite others to grow with you. This is the quiet, powerful work of thriving. It is not loud, but it lasts. It is not glamorous, but it changes lives.

Resilience in the Future

As you step into the future, remember that everything you have built so far is meant to evolve. The blueprint you hold is alive. It will grow with you as you grow, expanding to fit the person you are becoming. Each new experience adds to the design. Each new insight strengthens the structure. The aim is to improve what you have built, not to keep it as is. Thriving means tending to your life the way a master craftsman tends to his creation; with patience, presence, and reverence for the process.

There will still be days when the wind feels strong and the walls shake. There will still be seasons of uncertainty when you wonder if the work you have done will hold. In those moments, return to your foundation. Remember the lessons that steadied you before. You have already proven your ability to rebuild. You have learned that cracks do not mean collapse. They mean it is time to repair, reinforce, and grow again. You have built resilience into your very framework. You are stronger than you realize.

It is easy to forget that thriving is not about reaching a final stage of success. It is about the ongoing rhythm of rising, learning, resting, and beginning again. Each time you return to yourself after being tested, you deepen your wisdom. Each time you extend grace after pain, you expand your heart. You prove your ability to thrive by taking another step when quitting is easier. Every time you take one more step forward, you affirm your capacity to thrive. The beauty of this process is that it never truly ends. It continues for as long as you are alive, and every season adds a new dimension to the life you are creating.

Consider your current life as a living legacy. You are not merely existing, you are actively shaping your story. You are transforming your life into a lasting legacy. Your knowledge, beliefs, and healing all contribute to humanity's story. Your life becomes a chapter in the greater blueprint of human endurance and compassion. The more you grow, the more you contribute to that design. You are part of something larger than yourself. You are *both* student and teacher, builder *and* bridge.

When future generations look back, they will not remember you for the things you possessed. They'll remember how you inspired them to believe in the impossible, how you made them feel, and how you stood when it was easier to fall. They will carry forward the example you set. The lessons you live now will become the wisdom they lean on later. That is the quiet miracle of legacy. It outlives our years but never loses our essence.

Let your Blueprint be your message. Let your resilience become your signature. Let your kindness be your inheritance. You are already someone's blueprint for courage. You are proof that rebuilding is possible. You are already the light that someone else is looking for. The way you live matters more than you know.

As you continue on your journey, do not be afraid to start new chapters, to redesign what no longer fits, and to expand the rooms of your life to welcome new dreams. You have permission to continue building. You have permission to evolve. You have permission to become more than you ever imagined. Every experience you've had, every moment you've survived, has been preparing you for what comes next. You are not at the end. You are standing at a new beginning, carrying everything you have learned with you.

You have built a strong foundation rooted in truth. You have created a structure of values that keeps you grounded. You have filled your life with light through the windows of perspective and love. You have opened doors and doors and created pathways of opportunity, forgiveness, and faith. You have mended the fractures and cultivated the potential for growth. The house you have built is not just a reflection of your strength; it is a reflection of your heart. It holds the story of who you have been and the promise of who you are still becoming.

Your Open Door

As you walk through that house, notice the beauty in the details. Notice the way each wear mark has become a part of the design. Notice how every repaired corner tells a story of perseverance. Notice the light that filters through the spaces where you once saw only shadow. This is your creation. This is your life. You built it with resilience, with grace, and with faith in what could be. There is no greater achievement than that.

Now, take a moment to imagine who might one day walk through the doors of what you have built. A child, a friend, or a stranger inspired by your story. Imagine them finding shelter in your example, comfort in your honesty, and courage in your strength. That is the purpose of all this work. You are not only building for yourself. You are building for the world. You are building for those who will one day need to know that thriving is possible.

True leadership embodies a legacy in motion. It is the decision to rise each day and live as an example of what you believe in. It is the willingness to take responsibility for your influence and use it to uplift rather than diminish. It is the quiet understanding that every act of integrity, every moment of compassion, and every gesture of courage adds to the collective foundation of humanity. The world becomes stronger each time one person chooses to lead with heart.

So go forward with confidence in what you have built and faith in what you are still creating. Lead yourself with kindness. Teach through your actions. Inspire through your perseverance. Share your story generously so that others may find themselves within it. Let your life continue to be the living proof that from brokenness comes beauty, from uncertainty comes strength, and from endurance comes joy.

This is not the end of your story. It represents the continuation of a larger story. The blueprint is yours to refine, the tools are in your hands, and the world is waiting for the light only you can build. Step boldly toward what comes next. Build with courage. Live with clarity. Love with conviction. Keep expanding. Keep becoming. Keep thriving.

Because you were never simply meant to survive.

You were built to last.

You were built to lead.

You were *Built To Thrive*.

A Final Word

As I close these pages, I am reminded that resilience is never built alone.

Resilience, I have come to understand, is both inheritance and choice. We inherit the lessons, the values, and the quiet examples of those who came before us. Yet we must also choose, day by day, to keep building on that foundation. Resilience is formed in the stillness between life's major events, such as the gentle rustle of a morning newspaper, the warmth of a hand on your shoulder, or the well-known stories we tell long after the voices have faded.

My hardworking father taught me that strength can be gentle, work can be sacred, and love is the only architecture that truly lasts. Dad built homes, yes, but more importantly, he built us: a family rooted in trust, nurtured by laughter, and held together by the belief that we could weather any storm if we stood side by side.

I see my father's lessons taking root in new soil as I look at my grown children. The foundation he laid continues to hold us together because his legacy was built with love, patience, and an unwavering belief that we are stronger together than we could ever be apart.

Built to Thrive is more than just a story about one family. It is a living philosophy, a testament to how love, purpose, and perseverance can shape every generation that follows. The blueprint is simple, yet profound: work diligently, stay humble, keep your heart open, and never stop believing in the good that endures.

My father's legacy lives in every nail driven, every conversation shared, and every act of kindness that strengthens the structure of our lives. Now, as I pass the baton to my children and grand-children, I see the beauty of continuity. We strengthen what we've received, transforming resilience into something uniquely our own.

If you are looking for more generational wisdom, I invite you to join me on my Facebook™ Page, *Built to Thrive Living,* a page for stories, strength, and renewal. Here we explore what it means to build a positive life, one rooted in gratitude, resilience, and generational wisdom. Join me as I share reflections from *Built to Thrive*—**How to Use Generational Wisdom to Grow Your Resilience.**

If you are keen to learn more about reflections, along with everyday inspiration to help you slow down, reconnect, and keep building what matters most, then visit my website and come for the stories. Stay for the sense of belonging. www.builttothrive.living

I am always here for you should you desire to connect at: maryjo@builttothrive.living

May the days ahead serve as a reminder to seek your own blueprints in the people, the moments, and the values that keep you steady through life's challenges. May you honour what came before, build what is yours to create, and trust deeply in the process.

For you are you and you are built to thrive.

Coming Home

There are moments, often quiet and unplanned, when I still hear my father's voice. Sometimes it comes to me in the early morning light, when the world is still and the day has not yet begun. Other times it finds me when I am working, parenting, or simply thinking of him. It is never loud but always steady, a gentle reminder of all he taught me. His lessons were never about perfection or success. They were about presence, honesty, and care in the details. He believed that a life built with integrity will always stand, no matter the weather.

I look back now and understand that his lessons were never just for me. They were meant to be passed on, shaped by time, and carried forward through each generation. Every act of kindness, every quiet repair, every effort to keep building when life grows hard; these are the ways his voice continues to speak. It lives in me, and now, through these pages, it lives in you too.

That is how wisdom endures. It does not fade with the passing of years. It becomes part of the fabric of who we are, guiding us from within. Each of us holds a piece of someone else's story, a gift of guidance that we, in turn, are meant to share. This is the true legacy of thriving. It is not the house we build, but the light we leave in the windows for others to find their way home.

As you close this book, keep in mind and remember that your story continues to unfold and is still being written. Somewhere, someone is already learning from the way you live. They are watching how you rise after loss, how you speak with compassion, and how you keep faith when things are uncertain. They will remember your strength long after the details fade. That is how you lead. That is how you build something that lasts.

So go forward with the same care my father carried in his hands. Build slowly. Love deeply. Give generously. Let your life be both blueprint and beacon. And when you pause, when you rest, when you take in all that you have created, may you feel what I feel now, gratitude. Gratitude for the lessons that shaped you. Gratitude for the strength that sustains you. Gratitude for the wisdom that connects and unites us all across all time and across all generations.

You have come home to yourself. *And from that place of peace and purpose, may you continue to build, for yourself, for others, and for all those who will one day follow your blueprint.*

Much appreciation,
MJ

About the Author

Mary-Jo Bathe is a storyteller, writer, and advocate for resilience whose work explores how family legacies, values, and everyday wisdom shape the architecture of human experience. Drawing inspiration from her father, a Depression-era entrepreneur, home builder, and real estate developer, Mary-Jo weaves together themes of courage, love, and purpose across generations in her debut work, *Built to Thrive*.

Her writing combines memoir and reflection, transforming personal experience into universal insight. Through stories of laughter, loss, and perseverance, Mary-Jo reveals how the foundations we inherit, both tangible and emotional, become blueprints for the lives we continue to build. She writes with honesty and warmth, inviting readers to discover their resilience within quiet moments and enduring connections that define their identity and belonging.

Mary-Jo's professional background as a consultant in digital healthcare innovation and health IT transformation fostered her deep appreciation for planning, structure, systems, and human connection. The balance of precision and compassion she brought to modernizing healthcare now guides her storytelling, where every life, like every home, reflects design, purpose, and heart. Her career has shown her how true progress arises when innovation serves both design and the lives shaped by creative vision. A belief in purposeful creation anchors her narrative approach, where structure meets humanity, and resilience evolves into art.

Beyond the page, Mary-Jo is a mother, grandmother, and lifelong learner who believes that generational wisdom offers guidance in times of uncertainty. She finds joy in family gatherings, long walks in nature, rounds of golf with close friends, and daily rituals that ground her, such as morning coffee, shared meals, and stories retold until they become part of who we are.

Mary-Jo lives in Ontario, Canada, surrounded by family, nature, and the lasting echoes of her father's lessons. *Still building. Still learning. Still thriving.*

Book Resource List

- *How to Win Friends and Influence People* — Dale Carnegie
- *Anatomy of the Spirit* — Caroline Myss
- *Grounded Spirituality* —Jeff Brown
- *The Power of the Subconscious Mind* — Joseph Murray, PH.D., D.D.
- *Chasing Dreams* — Kobi Yamada
- *Astrology for the Soul* — Jan Spiller
- *Finding the Mother Tree, Discovering the Wisdom of the Forest* — Suzanne Simard
- *Healing Satori* — Dr. Ken W. Dick
- *Tales from a Seanchai* — Hugh S. Foley
- *Tuesdays with Morrie* — Mitch Albom

www.ingramcontent.com/pod-product-compliance
Lightning Source LLC
Chambersburg PA
CBHW051609120626
46551CB00014B/1733